'Last Orders'
Life as a Pub Landlord

'Last Orders'
Life as a Pub Landlord

Chris Pitts

ATHENA PRESS
LONDON

'Last Orders'
Life as a Pub Landlord
Copyright © Chris Pitts 2007

All Rights Reserved

No part of this book may be reproduced in any form
by photocopying or by any electronic or mechanical means,
including information storage or retrieval systems,
without permission in writing from both the copyright
owner and the publisher of this book.

ISBN 10-digit: 1 84748 029 2
ISBN 13-digit: 978 1 84748 029 3

First Published 2007 by
ATHENA PRESS
Queen's House, 2 Holly Road
Twickenham TW1 4EG
United Kingdom

Every effort has been made to protect the true identities of persons
alluded to in this text. All names of actual persons, living or dead,
events and locales have been changed, as well as the details of the
major events.

Printed for Athena Press

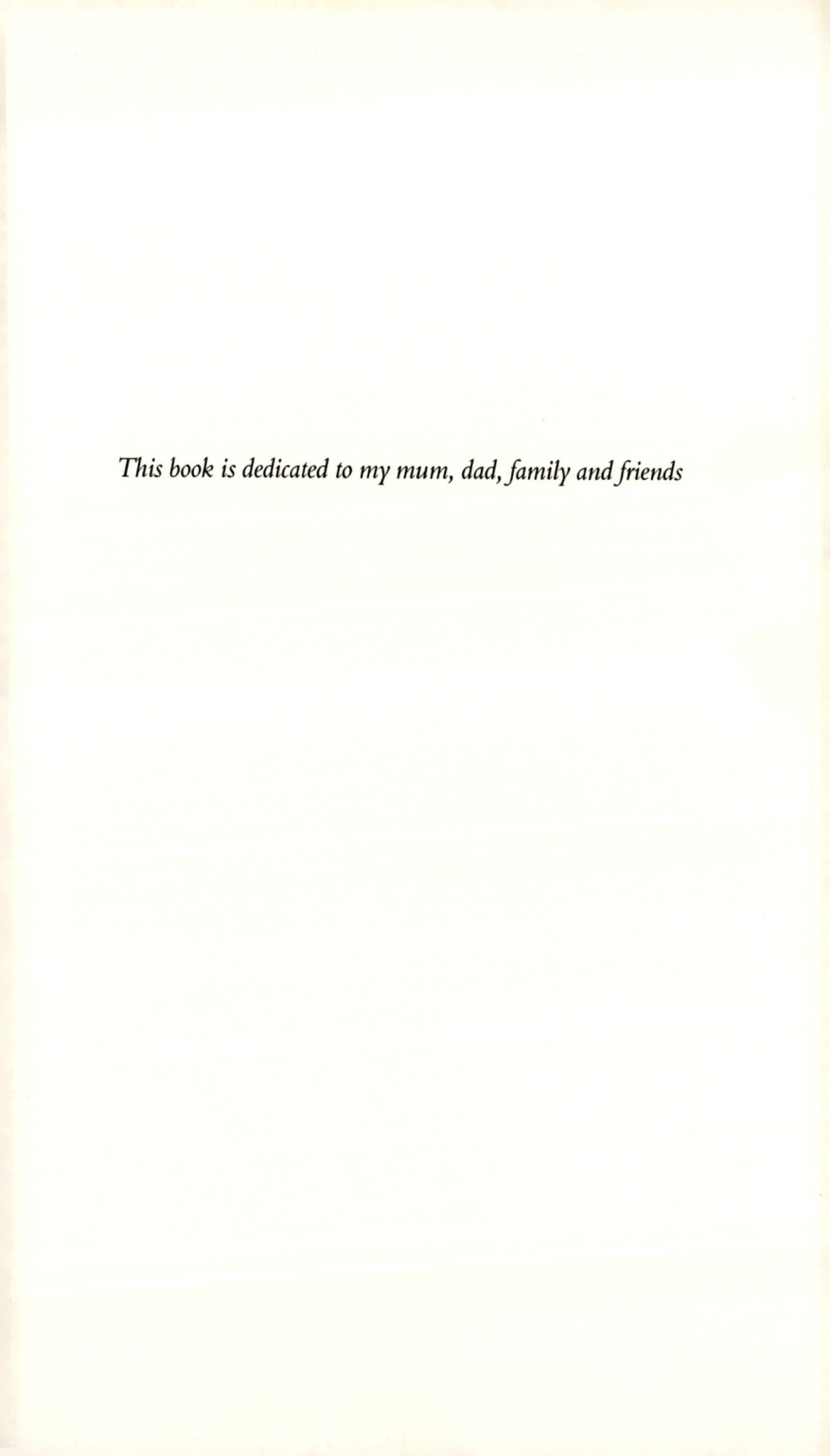

This book is dedicated to my mum, dad, family and friends

My thanks to everyone who has helped in any way towards getting this book published.

A special thank you to Francesca, as without your advice this book would never have been published.

Making Preparations

'Fancy popping over the road for a drink, Chris?' Michael asked me.

'Yeah, definitely,' I replied.

We headed over the road and into the wine bar opposite Lorien in Chertsey, where we were working at the time. We bought our drinks and sat down at the bar. I was feeling totally cheesed off, having just returned from two weeks in Spain.

'What made you move into the pub game, Derek?' we asked the owner, who was serving behind the bar.

'I wouldn't mind doing something like this,' I commented to Michael, after listening to Derek's story of how he had ended up running the place we were in. To be honest, at that moment, I felt like doing anything other than working in an office, which bored the pants off me.

'I'd love to as well,' agreed Michael.

'Have a look through this, then,' Derek suggested, tossing us a copy of that week's edition of the *Morning Advertiser*.

We were flicking through it until 'PUB IN HOUNSLOW' caught our eye.

'That's the Duke of Cambridge!' exclaimed Michael.

I had never been in the pub, although I had passed it thousands of times in my life, travelling to and from school. My only real memory of it was from when I was about sixteen. I had been standing outside when a Hounslow skinhead came up, accused me of seeing his bird behind his back and then proceeded to headbutt me. The chance would have been a fine thing, as I could not even speak to a girl at that age without going red. No sisters and attending an all-boys school contributed to that!

'Shall we give it a ring when we get back?' Michael asked enthusiastically.

'We can give it a bash,' I replied.

Michael and Scouse Steve, a mate of ours, went to have a look at the place and were very impressed with it. The following night, we climbed the back stairs and rang the bell at 8 p.m., as instructed by Alice, the landlady at the time.

The door opened and there in the dark stood a dead ringer for George Harrison during his 'My Sweet Lord' phase, with his long hair and beard.

'What do you want?' he demanded to know.

'Is Alice there, please?' I enquired.

'What do you want her for?' he asked aggressively. He was full of charisma, this bloke!

'I don't think that it's any of your business, do you?' I responded, trying rather unsuccessfully not to sound agitated.

After a few moments of our staring at each other, a pretty Spanish girl appeared alongside him.

'You are right. It is none of his business,' she agreed, giving him a dirty look. 'Alice went out a couple of hours ago and hasn't come back yet. Can I take a message for her?'

We met Alice a couple of times after that night and eventually took over the pub on 5 April 2000. However, by then there were four of us on board.

'How do you feel about Fitzy and Scouse Steve coming in as partners?' Michael had asked me.

'I don't mind; see what they say,' had been my reply.

They both agreed to join us in our new venture, so there were now four mates in it together. We were going to have a great social life, plenty of booze and fun, and also make some easy money in the meantime! What could possibly go wrong?

On 5 April 2000, we all arrived at the crack of dawn, full of enthusiasm in readiness for the opening party we were holding on Friday, 7 April. We worked hard all day, painting and cleaning (there was no keeping up with old George Chapman that day!) until early evening, when we sat down to have a few pints while watching Chelsea versus Barcelona on the big screen. It was a fantastic feeling, sitting in our own pub, having a few beers and watching a great match on our own private screen. In fact, we had more than a few drinks and ended up becoming well intoxicated. Baggott and Mick McGinty, two of the friends who had been helping us, were in a right state by the time we let them out to go home.

I sat down with Michael to have our last drink. After a few minutes, we heard a commotion outside and went to investigate. Two police officers had Baggott and Mick pinned against the shop opposite, where they were obviously questioning them. Baggott and Mick did not appear to be too pleased about this and were being completely uncooperative. They argued for what seemed like ages before being made to turn out their pockets. One of the officers fished something out of Baggott's pocket that appeared to be of real interest to him. He was holding it in his hand and, after further discussion, he crossed the road with Baggott in tow and marched towards the pub before banging loudly on the door.

'Do you recognise this?' asked the officer.

'Yes, it's our remote control,' we replied in unison.

'Well, we have just found it in this man's possession,' he explained, pointing at a bemused Baggott, who was standing alongside him. 'If you would like to press charges…'

However, Michael and I took one look at Baggott, standing there like a naughty schoolboy, and burst out laughing. The officers were not impressed.

'Do you mind telling me what is so funny?' asked the second officer, who had joined his colleague at the door.

'Nothing, really; it's just that…' We could not get the words out, as we were by then in complete stitches. We eventually managed to control our laughter.

'No, we don't want you to take any action this time,' we insisted.

'We hope that these are not the sort of shenanigans we are going to get from you lot here!' said one of the officers, to whom we had not given a very good first impression. We had not even opened yet and we already had a black mark against us!

On Friday, 7 April, we held our opening party by invitation only, so it was full of friends and relatives. It was packed with a brilliant atmosphere; we had a live band and my mum laid on a great spread. What a brilliant night!

The following morning, I marched to the bank to pay in the previous night's takings. We had made bundles on our first night. This pub game looked like it was going to be a piece of cake.

Fitzy Stamps his Authority

The following day was our official opening and most of Alice's regulars were there. It was Grand National Day, so we held a sweepstake, which was won by yours truly. 'Fix' was being shouted. I felt a bit awkward about winning it on the first day, so I handed the £60 winnings over the bar to buy a round for the regulars. The round came to over £80, so there I was over twenty quid down. That would teach me for winning the sweep!

The main group of regulars were congregated at the bar. They seemed to be in high spirits and were putting a lot of money over it, which was a good sign.

'Chris, are we going to allow dogs in?' asked Michael.

'Of course we are,' I replied indignantly. Michael must have suspected that that would be my answer, as would anybody who knew me.

After a while, the dog's owner, a big Geordie skinhead covered from head to toe in tattoos, began throwing beer mats for the dog to fetch. This continued for several minutes until he began throwing them onto a table where a middle-aged couple were sitting, having a drink. As usual, it was not the dog to blame, but the owner.

'Excuse me. Do you mind not doing that, as you are disturbing people?' Fitzy requested in his polite but firm manner. Fitzy was a tough, no-nonsense bloke from Glasgow who could more than look after himself.

'Fuck off, you Scottish prick!' was Geordie's response.

'OK, have it your way,' Fitzy replied, giving him that look that we all knew so well. They parted like two gunslingers in a Wild West showdown. Fitzy walked over to us, while Geordie went over to his mates, with a grin etched on his face as if he had scored the winning goal in the cup final. It was by no means the end of the situation and we knew it. Fitzy sat there quietly, trying to control his anger. After about ten minutes, Geordie walked past where we were sitting on his way to the toilet, giving Fitzy a triumphant look on the way. After about twenty seconds, Fitzy jumped out of his seat.

'Steve, come and stand outside the toilets and don't let anyone in,' he instructed.

Fitzy entered the Gents as Steve did as he was told and stood guard outside. Fitzy gave Geordie his best 'Glasgow kiss' and Geordie was not smiling any more as he lay in the urinals in a pool of blood.

'Do any of you want some as well?' Fitzy yelled at Geordie's drinking partners, who were congregated at the bar. None of them accepted his kind offer. Fitzy had already earned their respect.

Geordie had still not appeared after several minutes, so Fitzy returned to the toilets, reappeared with Geordie and frogmarched him to the door before hurling him onto the pavement outside. Geordie seemed reluctant to go and stayed hovering about the doorway.

'I'm going to really sort him out in a minute,' Fitzy growled, although we were under the impression that he already had.

'What about my dog?' Geordie pleaded when Fitzy ordered him away from the door.

'Oh, shit, I forgot about him,' responded Fitzy. 'What's his name?'

'Bonzo,' replied the dazed Geordie.

We were then treated to the hilarious sight of Fitzy crouching down, shouting, 'Bonzo, here, boy!' at the top of his voice as the bemused dog sat there, refusing to budge. So surreal, but it was just the start for us at the Duke of Cambridge.

Fitzy's head came in handy a few weeks later on a Friday afternoon, the day before Chelsea played Aston Villa in the FA Cup Final. I was upstairs, cleaning my teeth, when I heard one of the barmaids shouting for me:

'Chris, quick, Fitzy's fighting down here!'

I ran down the stairs as quickly as I could, not knowing how many were involved in this 'fight'. As I ran into the bar, I was greeted by the sight of Fitzy leaning over a big African bloke, who was sprawled out on the floor.

'You fuckin' bastard! I'll teach you threatening our customers.'
'What's going on, Fitz?' I asked.
'This bastard was threatening Alan and Ron,' he explained. Alan and Ron were two old boys who used to prop up the bar.

Fitzy was attempting to drag him out of the bar, but the man had wrapped his legs around the base of a table. I untangled his legs, grabbed his ankles and helped Fitzy to lift him into the air. It looked as if we were about to give him the bumps! We carried him to the door and threw him out into the street. He picked himself up and I noticed that he had blood all over his face. As with lots of bullies, he was probably shocked that someone had stood up to him.

A group of blacks was passing at that moment, and they were all looking with great interest at what was going on.

'They have just attacked me and beaten me up!' our troublemaker shouted at the group.

'Like fuck! The bastard was threatening old people in the pub and got what he deserved,' I retorted.

The group weighed up the situation before giving their verdict:

'That's out of order, starting on old people!' shouted one.

'You got what you deserved!' yelled another in agreement.

The following day was Cup Final Day and we had an early start. People started arriving at the pub from 7 a.m. onwards for an early drink before setting off for Wembley. There was even an open-top Routemaster bus with 'Wembley' on the front leaving the pub at noon, organised by Ernie, a Chelsea fan of many years. There were Bone, Nef, General, Neilson, Dave Cooper, Steve Cook, Chris Cottle and their lot, Oz, Alex, Rhys and co. and Mark and Darren Nicholls, Lee and Dean Hanshaw, Andy Edwards and Darren Chaffy from Bedfont. Everyone was in high spirits. 'Lola' by the Kinks was blasting out of the jukebox, although to a man, everyone was shouting 'Zola' whilst drinking pints of beer and tucking into bacon sandwiches. The door was still locked, as we were not allowed to open officially until 11 a.m. Suddenly, there was somebody peering through the window, gesturing angrily at me. I walked to the door and, as I unlocked it, I realised it was our African 'mate' from the previous day. I stepped out into the street, while he continued shouting.

'My nose is fuckin' broken! What did he fuckin' do that for?' he demanded to know.

'Cause you threatened some old boys at the bar, that's why,' I replied.

'I didn't mean it. I wasn't going to do anything,' he continued, shouting at the top of his voice. Suddenly, Fitzy appeared and our 'mate' was off up the road faster than Ben Johnson on speed, never to be seen again.

Michael, Michelle and the Police Raid

The first couple of months went quite well, on the whole, although, for obvious reasons, Euro 2000 was a disappointment, with the exception of the opening twenty minutes of the England versus Portugal game and England's victory against Germany.

We had a couple of pool teams, a darts team and a football team up and running and had already enjoyed some mad nights. One major problem, though, was Michael being such a dirty bastard. His own personal hygiene was not a problem, but he would leave the kitchen and bathroom in a terrible mess. This problem multiplied when his girlfriend, Michelle, moved in, as she was twice as dirty as him.

As I already mentioned, I had, with the help of a mate called Oz, started a pub team. Oz knew loads of people and, over the course of the next couple of years, he introduced loads of players to the pub. In our second season, we won the league and got to the Cup Final, only to lose 3–1 against a team we had done the double over in the league that season. One evening, after training, some of us went back to the pub for a couple of drinks, as per usual. After a couple of hours, Oz, Alex and the rest of the boys started drifting off home before I started chatting to a lovely girl who I shall call Emma. She was a friend of one of the barmaids. We had a few drinks and were getting on really well. Michael kept supplying us with drinks, and that was helping my chances with Emma. However, there was a reason for Michael's generosity. My mum had been doing the cooking for the pub, but she had that day walked out because she could no longer stand the filthy state Michael and Michelle were leaving it in. Michael's latest present for Michelle was a Labrador puppy, although the idiots had no idea of what was involved in looking after a puppy. They never took her out for a walk and, when the poor dog messed on the carpet, they would step over it without cleaning up the mess. I was on the verge of blowing my top and Fitzy knew it.

'This is going to be a big problem, Michael, if you don't clean up your act,' he scolded him.

'Yeah, I know; don't worry, I will,' Michael replied.

Michelle was pulling the strings and Michael was dancing to her tune. 'Michelle has so much experience, we should make her manager,' was one of his typical comments.

I was at boiling point and Michael knew it. He was trying to butter me up and, what better way is there to calm a bloke down than by helping him to get fixed up with a beautiful girl who, under normal circumstances, he probably would not have had a chance with? Therefore, although I knew what Michael was up to, I wanted to enjoy the moment with Emma, so the other business could wait until the next day.

Emma stayed the night, but the enjoyment of being with her was rudely interrupted in the early hours of the morning:

'Open the door now; police!' somebody shouted, bashing on the door.

'What do they want?' asked Emma.

'God knows, but I'm sure it's not a drink,' I replied as I jumped out of bed. I pulled on a pair of tracksuit bottoms and a tee shirt whilst our alarm clock in uniform continued thumping on the door:

'Come on, open this door now!'

'What the f—?'

'Christopher Michael Neil Pitts, you are under arrest for defrauding Lorien plc out of the sum of £250,000. Anything you do or say will be taken down and may be used in evidence against you,' or words to that effect were uttered by the officer.

An attractive woman entered the room, and it quickly became obvious that she was the boss of this operation. There was a lot of activity along the corridor, with numerous officers in uniform as well as a few in plain clothes charging about. I stood there, trying to take it all in.

'We have a warrant to search the whole premises,' I was informed.

'In that case, I don't suppose there's any chance of me having a shower while you're doing that, is there?' I asked, expecting a sharp rebuff.

'Yes, so long as it's a quick one,' Maxine Cilia, the CID boss, surprisingly replied.

As I headed for the bathroom, armed with a towel, I spotted Michael, looking very worried.

Fortunately, the male officer waited outside the bathroom. If an officer were going to accompany me in there, I would have had to insist on it being Ms Cilia!

Whilst showering, I was wondering what Michael could have done with the cash.

'250 grand and you've never said a word,' I muttered to myself. I knew that he had been flying with Michelle to Cork and back business class, but that would have only made a small dent in a quarter of a million quid.

After my shower, I walked back to my room and got dressed. Emma was brushing her hair in the mirror and had taken it all in her stride. In fact, she looked as if she did not have a care in the world.

'Do us a favour and keep it quiet for me?' I asked her. How many females could keep something like that quiet? To her great credit, she did not even tell her best friend.

I grabbed a book to read in the cell, as I had gathered by then that it was not going to be a flying visit to the station. They were still searching through all my belongings.

'Is this yours?' asked one of the coppers, holding a CS Gas canister.

About ten minutes later, another one pulled out a lump of cannabis from my jeans. 'Is this yours as well?' Things were getting worse!

'I've got to put these on you,' one of them announced, suddenly producing a set of handcuffs.

'No way! I'm not having those put on me,' I protested.

'I'm afraid I've got no choice,' he insisted.

For the first time that morning, I was beginning to get really fed up with it all. I had done nothing wrong and yet the police had raided the pub, had searched it from top to bottom, had been through all my personal possessions and now, to cap it all, they wanted to handcuff me.

'You have to have these on. You are under arrest.'

'No way! I'm under the hospital for neck and spinal injuries, so there's no way I'm having those put on me.'

He looked at Maxine Cilia, who looked at me before looking back at him.

'OK, leave him,' she instructed.

'Right, we'll let you come with us without them, but, if you try anything stupid, we'll come down on you like a ton of bricks,' he warned.

'I won't be making a run for it and I won't be doing anything stupid because I haven't done anything wrong,' I replied.

He gave me one of those 'I've heard it all before' looks. I was taken out and put into a police car. Michael had been put into a different one. All the police cars were lined up outside the pub. What a great advert for us! The hairdressers from the parlour opposite, the other shopkeepers and the bus drivers from the garage next door had all come to watch the fun.

We arrived at the station about half an hour later. I can not recall whether it was Addlestone or Woking, but I attended both of them.

After having my possessions taken from me, I was led to my cell. Fortunately, they had allowed me to take my book with me, so I settled down to read it. It was a Spanish grammar book. However, I am sure that most people who have been in a cell will probably say the same thing: it is impossible to concentrate on anything, as your mind keeps drifting off to the reason why you are there. A cell is a lonely, boring, smelly, claustrophobic place.

For the first time, I realised that it was not only Michael and I who had been arrested in connection with the investigation, but Michael's ex-girlfriend Debbie as well. She had worked in the same office as us at Lorien the previous year.

'But what about my daughter?' I could hear her protesting. 'She needs to be picked up from nursery.'

'Is there anybody known to the nursery staff who could pick her up?' asked a policewoman.

'The only person I can think of at the moment is Michael's girlfriend, Michelle,' replied Debbie.

She was allowed to make a phone call to the nursery. Lying on my 'bed' in my cell, I could hear her explaining the situation to the nursery staff. How must she have felt at that moment, having to ask the woman her partner had left her for to do her the favour of picking up her daughter from the nursery? Debbie was not really my cup of tea and I am sure that I was not really hers either, but I felt really sorry for her at that moment.

After the telephone conversation, it went quiet again. I was staring at the Spanish verb tables in my book but was unable to absorb any information. Suddenly, there were footsteps approaching. When you are stuck in a cell, you are always hopeful that it is you they are coming for. Even if it is only for questioning, at least it breaks the monotony for a while. The keys rattled as they found their way into the lock and my cell door flew open.

'Right, follow me,' the officer instructed. I followed him down the corridor and into an interview room, where Maxine Cilia and a colleague were waiting. They went through the usual procedures before beginning the interview.

'Margaret is convinced you were the ringleader,' revealed Ms Cilia. Margaret had been our boss at Lorien.

'Is she?' I asked, smiling.

'What is so amusing?' she asked.

'It's just that she hated my guts,' I explained. She also thought the sun shone out of Michael's backside, but that was not for me to say.

'How well do you know Fitzy?' she asked. That was a question that I had not expected.

'I don't,' I replied.

'Are you sure?'

'Of course I'm sure. I don't know anyone by that name,' I insisted.

'In that case, how do you explain his name being in your address book under several contact numbers and it also being stored on your mobile?' Maxine Cilia enquired enthusiastically as she produced an address book and mobile, which were both clearly mine. Fitzy was changing his address and phone number so frequently that the page under the letter 'F' was the most full in the book.

Shit, I didn't think of that! I thought to myself. They continued scrutinising me impatiently, waiting for me to explain myself.

'Which Fitzy are you talking about?'

'Why, how many do you know?' they asked in surprise.

'Several,' I replied.

'That's funny; you didn't know any just now!' the male colleague chipped in.

'I've worked with a few, played football with a few; I've—'

'Were any of them called Martin Fitzwater?' he interrupted, beginning to lose his patience.

'I wouldn't know. I only knew them all as Fitzy.'

The conversation continued going round in circles until they obviously realised that they were not getting anything about him from me. They would have no doubt already tried all the numbers listed under the name 'Fitz' in my address book and on my mobile, although Fitzy would have been tipped off by then.

They moved on to question me about my role at Lorien before suddenly producing a set of keys.

'Do you recognise these?'

'Of course I do. They're from my flat. How did you get them, or shouldn't I ask?'

'I haven't been round there, but some of our team have. Unfortunately, they had to force their way in.'

'I don't suppose it would have occurred to you to ask me for a key?' I asked, although I knew that that would have greatly reduced their job satisfaction. In all fairness, she was as nice as somebody could be in those circumstances. I was led back to my cell, where I was kept until almost midnight.

The following day, I went to my flat in Chiswick and was horrified by what greeted me there. The police, behaving like hooligans, had smashed my door in, ripped out the bath, spilt paint over my records, and left it in a right mess. I was livid and took photos of the damage they had done, but, despite making a formal complaint and pursuing it for a couple of years, I did not get anything, not even an apology. The wrong class and religion, I presume.

Michael could not care less what had happened to my flat. Fitzy apologised and insisted that they would pay for a new door and for the damage, but they never paid a penny.

Fitzy in Further Trouble

It was not long after these events that Fitzy decided he needed to get out of the business, as he was getting into too much trouble. Although Michael did not want to go, I decided that it was time for him and his unhygienic girlfriend to go as well, in order to enable us to make a fresh start.

Apart from the two aforementioned fights that Fitzy had had, there were about another ten punch-ups, including one with me where we ended up rolling around amongst the beer crates at 3 a.m. Some of the others ran out the back to break it up, although I admit that he got the better of me, as the two black eyes he had given me verified. Mind you, the next day, he was complaining to me that I had done a little bit of damage to his head by hitting him with a beer crate. We concocted a bizarre story of how I had fallen down the cellar stairs before hitting my head and face on a beer keg. Apart from those who had witnessed our disagreement, we thought it would be better to cover up what had happened. We need not have bothered going to all that effort, because I found out later that everybody put two and two together immediately.

The following morning, I played football in a good friend, Nobby's, memorial match, which we hold every year, and, of course, I stuck to the same story in the dressing room before the match. However, they also all guessed what had really occurred, although they did not say anything at the time.

A couple of weeks after our set-to, I went out one Sunday night and so can only give the witnesses' version of events:

There were six people drinking at the bar coming up to last orders, but for some reason Fitzy had it in for Mick McGinty that night. Mick was Irish and could be very argumentative when he had had a few drinks, although I had always got on well with him. By all accounts, he was sitting, having a drink and chatting with the others, when Fitzy started to single him out.

'Let me have your glass now, Michael.' He would always call somebody by their full name when he was being serious.

'Aye, Fitzy,' responded Mick.

'I mean right now, Michael,' Fitzy persisted.

'OK, Fitz, one minute,' Mick replied, taking another mouthful of his pint.

'Right, you've had your chance!' growled Fitzy as he grabbed the pint with one hand and punched Mick with the other. The others broke it up and Mick left and went straight over the road to get a kebab.

'Who have you been fighting with?' asked the man serving behind the counter.

'What do you mean?' demanded Mick.

'Look in the mirror; you're bleeding.'

After looking in the mirror, Mick charged out of the shop without his kebab and stormed over the road and straight through the public bar. He then charged like a bull at Fitzy, who was standing behind the bar, holding an inquest with the other Michael into the original incident. Unfortunately, Fitzy was no matador, so he was unable to sidestep Mick in time and therefore took the full force of Mick's head in his chest, knocking him to the floor. Fitzy had been taken totally by surprise and Mick took the opportunity to get a few digs in. However, Fitzy soon managed to turn the tables and got on top of Mick, strangling him while continuously punching him with the other hand. The others, minus Michael, who stood there doing nothing, realised that Mick was receiving a severe beating, so they attempted to pull Fitzy off him, but without success, as Fitzy was by this time in a frenzy. Fortunately, Simon, a big rugby-playing regular who was a real gentleman, stepped in, so they were finally able to pull him off. However, by the time they succeeded, Fitzy had really done Mick some serious damage. It is probably not too much of an exaggeration to say that they probably saved his life.

'Mick, what are you doin' sleepin' there?' Harry asked after entering the living room of his flat, where Mick was staying for a while.

'Mick, come on,' Harry shouted with a bit more urgency. Mick was lying on the settee, making strange gurgling noises.

Harry turned him over and realised that he had been choking on his own blood. He rushed him to hospital to get him some urgent medical attention.

Harry is Scouse Steve's brother and both are equally nice blokes, although Harry has got a far shorter fuse than Steve. Steve was on his way to work the next morning when he received a call on his mobile from Harry:

'Where's that fucker Fitzy?'

'What's up, Harry? Calm down.'

'Calm down? Calm down? He's given McGinty a right hiding!'

'Don't get involved, Harry. You know what Mick can be like when he's had a drink,' Steve said, attempting to pacify the irate Harry.

'I fuckin' know what he can be like, but nobody deserves that!' Harry screamed down the phone.

Harry swears that, if he had found Fitzy at that moment, he would have killed him. Fitzy went back to Glasgow to lie low for a while. After the dust had settled, he returned once again to stay at the pub and was making a real effort to be more relaxed. To be fair, he was normally great fun socially, but he could fly off the handle without any warning.

The following Friday night, I felt confident enough to go out without worrying too much. Besides, Scouse Steve was there and he was always a calming influence on everyone.

'I'm off. Try not to give anyone that Glasgow kiss of yours, Fitzy!' I yelled out as I was leaving.

'Whip, my days of fighting are over. I've turned over a new leaf now.' He really meant it, just like George Best meant it whenever he vowed to give up the drink. 'Whip' was a nickname I had had for many years and despite what Swanny claims, it had nothing whatsoever to do with the Reeperbahn in Hamburg!

I returned home that night and came round the back way. One of the great advantages of having a pub is that you can always round off the night by downing a few pints as a nightcap. As I walked towards the back door, I was surprised to see Steve and Fitzy in a deep discussion. They both looked up as they heard me approaching.

'Are you off somewhere, Fitzy?' I enquired, noticing the suitcase in his hand.

They both looked at me awkwardly. I could sense that they wanted to tell me something but did not know how to, so I broke the ice.

'Who have you hit this time, Fitz?' I asked in a chirpy voice. When something happens as regularly as a postman delivering post, you tend not to be too surprised by it.

'Well, I lost it with these two Sri Lankans here tonight... oh, Whip, I can't stay here anymore. I'm going to stay in a hotel tonight and go back to Glasgow tomorrow.'

I felt sorry for him at that moment. The one thing he could not be accused of was being a bully, as he always stood up against bullies (remember Geordie?).

'Come on, don't be stupid. Let's go inside and have a drink.' He could have killed half a dozen customers, and yet all I cared about at that moment was having a few more drinks. I also knew how he felt, as I am no angel and there have been a few occasions in my life when I have had to reflect on things I have done, especially after drinking too much.

The three of us went inside to have a drink, and Steve and Fitzy filled me in on the evening's events. There had been some tension in the public bar between a couple of Sri Lankans and two Afghans. To be honest, the Sri Lankans in the area were generally no problem whatsoever. As often is the case, the friction was over a girl, and it resulted in one of the Sri Lankans threatening one of the Afghans with a pool cue. Fitzy and Steve intervened and told the two Sri Lankans to leave. They did not want to, but Fitzy could be very persuasive in these situations. They evicted the two of them and came back into the pub. Suddenly, there was a loud smash, with glass shattering everywhere. The bastards had put the window in.

Fitzy charged out of the door and up the road after them, but he had no chance of catching them as, even many years before, when playing football as a very accomplished midfielder, he had no speed. Steve, though, was a bit faster and managed to catch up with one of them by the tube station. In the duration of the scuffle, a huge bread knife fell to the ground. 'Keep him away from me!' one of the Sri Lankans was yelling, obviously petrified of Fitzy. He managed to struggle free and ran off up the road with his friend, so Steve and Fitzy returned to the pub with the knife and began clearing the glass up. It was almost closing time, so Steve locked the door.

Suddenly, the Sri Lankan who had dropped the bread knife popped his head through the broken window and asked, in complete seriousness, 'Excuse me, I'm a Tamil Tiger; can I have my knife back?'

'What did you fuckin' say?' demanded Fitzy, who hated knives of any sort.

'I said I'm a Tamil Tiger; can I have my knife back?' he repeated, just as seriously.

'Steve, unlock this door right now; I'm really gonna sort this bastard out!' Fitzy ordered him, almost foaming at the mouth.

They charged out of the door again in hot pursuit of the two Sri Lankans, and somehow Steve managed to catch up with them again. It must have been all those games of squash Steve and I played together, where I would have him running all over the court! This time, the other bloke dropped a bread knife almost identical to the first one. Fitzy by then was absolutely furious and they were off like a shot, but they were wise enough on this occasion not to return and ask for their knife back.

The action was not quite over for the evening yet, as Fitzy was totally worked up by then. When one customer called Sonny failed to drink up when requested by Fitzy, he got smacked in the chops. Fitzy then turned to his mate, who had also stood up, and asked him the question, 'Do you want some as well?'

Steve managed to calm him down and got the two customers to leave. This was about an hour before I met up with Steve and Fitzy at the back door.

We had a few drinks at the bar and Fitzy calmed down a lot. The following day was Saturday and, during the afternoon, Sonny walked in with two mates. He was not stupid enough to have come in looking for trouble, or he and his two friends would have got hurt. He asked if he could speak to Fitzy out the back in private, which did not concern me a great deal, as there would have only been one winner if Sonny had started anything. After about ten minutes, the pair of them came back into the pub and Sonny then asked if he could speak to me in private. We went out the back to where he had just been with Fitzy.

'Your friend has apologised, so the matter is now resolved. I will not be taking any further action,' he explained, sounding like a police inspector.

I did not like the bloke, in fact, I detested him, as he was a sneaky, arrogant bastard, but he could have made things difficult for us. Not in a trouble way, but he was the sort whose dad would have been a councillor and whose five brothers would all have been barristers. He was always coming into the pub, producing expensive clothing from numerous bags and announcing to everyone how much each item had cost. However, despite my dislike for the pretentious prick, I had to accept that he was behaving decently over this.

'That's good of you,' I replied. 'Come inside and I'll buy you a drink,'

He followed me back into the pub and I bought him a couple of drinks. Unfortunately, I then had to stand and listen to him talking nonsense for the next half an hour, but I knew it was worth the price. Not long after this incident, Sonny emigrated. He went to Canada, and as far as I was concerned, the Canadians were welcome to him.

A couple of months later, Steve, Fitzy and I were having a drink with a few of the regulars when the conversation turned to Sonny. I heard someone in the group say something about paying Sonny.

'What's that about paying him?' I demanded to know.

Everybody stood there in an awkward silence until Fitzy explained, 'Oh, Whip, I didn't want you to know 'cause I know what you're like. I paid him some money to keep him quiet.'

'Paid him some money; how much?'

'A hundred quid?'

'A hundred fuckin' quid!' I repeated in astonishment.

'Whip, you have to understand I did it for you and the pub, as I didn't want what I had done to come back and harm the business.'

'That fuckin' bastard, he stood there taking drinks off me

while I was saying how decent he had been.' I ranted. If Sonny had walked into the pub at that moment, I would have attacked him there and then.

'That's why I didn't want you to know, Whip,' Fitzy explained, justifying his actions.

Fitzy therefore decided to get out of the business, as he knew it was impossible for him to keep his temper in check under stress.

Eighteen months later, Fitzy was sentenced to twenty-one months' imprisonment, while Michael, being the inside man, received twenty-four months for the Lorien fraud case.

The Right Honourable Sir Gerard Morley

After reading these events, you may be thinking that our time at the Cambridge was only full of fights and arguments, but that was not the case at all. There were so many characters drinking in the pub, so many occurrences; some happy, some sad and some incredible. Many years ago, my mum would be watching *EastEnders* or *Coronation Street* and there would always be something happening in the Queen Vic or the Rovers. I would frequently make the comment, 'As if all that would happen in one pub!' I had to eat those words many times during my six years at the Duke, as I realised how much more could actually occur in one pub and did in the Duke of Cambridge. The pub had a right mix of characters over the years.

'Imagine a fly-on-the-wall documentary on this lot!' General would often comment. 'People wouldn't believe that people like this really exist.' 'General' is the nickname that my brother Mark has had since the seventies, due to his being a great organiser, especially for Chelsea away games.

If a programme were based on the regulars, I think it could be sensational, although the viewers would probably think that some of the characters were exaggerated. However, it is impossible to exaggerate some of them, as they were as eccentric or as unique as you could possibly get. Let us take Ged, for example, who was a dead ringer for Andy Capp. He always wore a flat cap and glasses and was a typical Yorkshireman, as tight as you could get, argumentative and so bad at telling jokes he made Tony Blackburn sound like a stand-up comedian. Ged was a bus driver whose problem was that his 'Flo' was as hard as nails. She came into the pub on a few occasions, poured Ged's pint away and marched him out of the door and home. Ged would be in tears; not through being humiliated, as he was too thick-skinned for that, but because some of his pint had been tipped away! His wife was from the Philippines, and Gurmit, another regular, would often quip. 'Most blokes who bring a wife back from Thailand or the Philippines get one who does everything for them, but Ged brings one back who bosses him about!'

We could not believe it when Ged told us how his wife had insisted that he could under no circumstances whatsoever let her relatives in the Philippines know that he was 'only' a bus driver. She insisted that he must keep up the pretence of being the local mayor, so he is known out there to this day as 'The Right Honourable Sir Gerard Morley'! Ged, I apologise if your relatives ever read this book and find out the truth, but I think being a bus driver is nothing to be ashamed of. In fact, after being a bus driver for so long in an area like Harlesden, I think you deserve a medal!

Whenever there was football showing in the pub, Ged would cheer on the opposing team to the majority, yelling out ridiculous comments such as, 'Come on! You can do it if you B&Q it!' at crucial points in the match. How no one throttled him, I do not know. To be honest, Harry nearly did on more than one occasion.

Ged's wife often ordered him to go to the local supermarket, and he was always happy to obey her, as, after doing the shopping, he would use the opportunity to pop into the pub for a quick pint on the way home. Invariably, that pint would always become five, six or even more, although Ged generally only paid for one or two of those. He would drive the regulars mad by scrounging drinks and cigarettes off them all the time, although he would appease them by running errands, such as, for example, going over to the shop to buy their fags for them or running to the bookies to place their bets.

One of Ged's main weaknesses was that, after a few drinks, he would take his eye off his shopping bags, a fatal mistake in the Cambridge. On many occasions, food would disappear from his shopping bags and then reappear on the bar for hungry regulars. Sausage sandwiches, jacket potatoes and hot cross buns were all provided at some time or another by Ged without his knowledge! The scene must have been hilarious when, several hours after being sent out for sausages, he returned without any in his bags.

Ged was one of those people who loved nothing more than getting something for nothing. Therefore, when these snacks were put on the bar, he would often comment, 'That's very kind of you,' not realising that he was stuffing his face with his own food! Suddenly, everyone's opinion of Ged would change; he was not a tight-fisted Yorkshireman after all, but a generous bloke providing food for everyone!

One Saturday night, after Ged had been in the pub for about seven or eight hours, General and Tiziana (better known as Banana, our crazy but popular Italian barmaid) placed about ten empty bottles of beer amongst his shopping. Ged described to us how, when he arrived home, his impatient and angry wife was waiting for him, so she discovered that the chicken she had intended to cook for dinner had turned into six empty bottles of Corona Extra and four bottles of Light Ale. Ged explained how he had had to beg her to prevent her from storming into the pub to sort us all out. 'They are making a fool out of you, Gerry,' she would scold him.

Incidentally, Malcolm, Big Mark, Kirpal and some of the other regulars polished off the chicken the next day.

One Saturday in September, it was Norma's birthday. Norma was a funny and likeable Irish lady of about fifty, who worked with people who had mental health problems.

'The people in here are madder than the people at work!' she would frequently comment.

As with all the regulars, we had got Norma a birthday cake. Tiziana lit the candles and brought the cake out as we sang 'Happy Birthday.' Norma was delighted and turned to walk away.

'Don't go yet, Norma,' I bellowed on the microphone. 'We've had a whip-round for you and would like to present it to you now.'

Ged leant forward and shouted in Gurmit's ear. 'If I'd known you were having a whip-round for Norma, I'd have chipped in.'

'Don't worry, Ged, you already have!' quipped Gurmit.

'No, I haven't...' protested Ged.

'Here you are, Norma. This is from all your friends in the pub!' I announced, handing the gift to Norma.

'Thank you, Chris. This is wonderful!' Norma shouted into the microphone.

'Hey, that's my cheese!' Ged yelled suddenly, noticing that the big, round, yellow object I had just presented Norma with was the same cheddar he had bought a couple of hours previously. 'Give it back!' he demanded, trying to wrestle it from Norma.

'No, Ged, let go! You're not having it, it's my birthday present!' insisted a deadly serious Norma, tightening her grip on the cheese.

A tug of war followed, which Norma, being the stronger of the two, won. Ged made another attempt to grab it, but Norma sidestepped him and threw it rugby-style to Gurmit, who promptly caught it and dived, placing the 'ball' on the floor as if scoring a try at Twickenham! Now, if you picture that, Gurmit is a big bloke of about eighteen stone. On his thirty-sixth birthday, a few of us brave idiots decided to give him the bumps and, despite having strong blokes like Scottish John and Malcolm in the group the counting went something like as follows.

'One, two, three, four, five, six, seven... eight... nine... thirty-three... thirty-four... thirty-five... thirty-six and...'

We did not quite manage the 'one for luck'. Where were you when you were needed, Big Mark? Big Mark was the strongest in the pub by far.

Anyway, to get back to the stolen cheese, Ged gave in and joined the rest of us in laughter as Gurmit and Norma played football with it. They then rifled through Ged's shopping to produce a swede, which they placed on the pool table and attempted to pot; an impossible task, seeing as it was twice the size of the pockets!

'I've always wanted to poke a Swede in the hole!' commented Gurmit.

Later on that night, Norma was dancing with her friends, Di, Nichola and Banana, when I played 'Some Girls' by Racey. The girls were all singing along to the lyrics;

'Some girls will, some girls won't
'Some girls need a lot of loving and some girls don't...'
when Norma piped up, 'I certainly don't!'

Ricardo.com

Ged was not the only person to have his food stolen. Anyone who ordered food in the pub and took their eye off it for a moment would find half a dozen chips and a bite of their hamburger missing. Malcolm was always a real predator as far as food was concerned and was very quick to pounce when the opportunity arose.

Ged always took it very well, unlike his mate and sparring partner Richard, sometimes known as 'Ricardo' thanks to Federico; he was a Dick Dastardly lookalike, so 'Richard' was an appropriate name for him. I used to drive him mad by singing 'Ricardo.com' to him to the tune of the 'Ocado' advert whenever he entered the pub.

'I wish you would stop singing that whenever I come in!' he snapped at me one evening, when he was in a particularly grumpy mood. Once he made that comment. I could not help myself and had to sing it to him every time he came into the pub. It was a lottery as to how he would take it, depending on what sort of day he had had and what sort of mood he was in when entering the pub. He would either chuckle away or give me a filthy look and read his newspaper for the next hour, only speaking when ordering a pint. He was a Scot whose mother was Welsh. He was always being wound up by Malcolm, Scottish John, Kirpal and Gurmit about shagging sheep, but he normally took it well. The one thing he was guaranteed to react to was any criticism of the London Underground, where he was employed as a station supervisor at Paddington.

A few of the boys from the pub had witnessed him in action at work and could not believe how authoritarian he was. Omar, a big 6'7" West Ham fan from Canning Town who had moved over to our side of London, often told how Richard would refuse to let anyone through without a ticket even when the ticket office and machines were out of action.

Kirpal loved telling the story of how Richard had refused to let an elderly lady take her poodle on the escalator, insisting that she had to use the steps instead. Whenever Kirpal reminded Richard of this by shouting across the bar at him, Ricardo would respond by yelling, 'Health and Safety! Health and Safety!'

When two Spanish friends of mine, Fifi-Lauren and David, came into the pub one night, I told Richard they needed advice on how to get around London and asked him if he could advise them on which ticket they needed. They were stuck with him telling them the price of every ticket and which tube they should get to every famous place in London for the next hour, while I tried to make them laugh by making faces behind Richard's back.

If anyone ever moaned about bus fares, God help them, because Richard would suddenly produce half a dozen leaflets on Oyster cards and lecture the person complaining about all the benefits of having an Oyster card, and yet he had not been a bus driver for years. Richard was absolutely potty about Shania Twain and would put every track of her Greatest Hits on the jukebox on his pay day. He would bombard me with requests for me to put on anything by her when I was playing the music, and when I finally gave in and played one of her tracks, he would charge onto the dance floor and stamp his feet with such ferocity that it seemed like only a matter of time until he would go through the floorboards and land in the cellar!

For several years, Richard had an on-off affair with Norma that made Den and Angie's relationship in *EastEnders* seem uneventful and stable. One particular Monday evening, I was having a drink with my mate, Billy, with whom I have been mates since school, when there was a commotion at the bar.

'Norma's just clumped Richard!' exclaimed Billy.

'You're joking.'

'She's gonna hit him again,' Billy predicted and, at that precise moment, Norma jumped off her stool and punched Richard with a full blow to the back of the head. She got even angrier as Richard sat there without flinching, and punched him four or five times with a combination that Sugar Ray Leonard would have been proud of!

'I'd better go and sort it out, Bill,' I said, as I made my way over to where they were at the end of the bar. Norma was shouting obscenities at Richard, who was sitting, there staring ahead and refusing to react, although, looking back, I am sure he was thriving on being the centre stage in this drama.

'You bastard!' Norma screamed as she punched him with a right-hander, and she was about to follow up with a left-hander when I grabbed her.

'Come on, Norma, leave it.'

'Chris, let me... he's a bastard.'

'All right, Norma, let's go,' I said, guiding her towards the exit.

I got her to the door, which was no mean feat, when she blurted out, 'Chris, I've left my shopping in there.'

'All right Norma, I'll go and get it for you. Wait there.'

'Are you OK, Richard?' I asked as I collected Norma's shopping for her. She seemed to have about ten bags of it.

'Yes, I'm fine,' Richard reassured me. However, he had just finished getting the words out of his mouth when he received another massive blow to the head.

'Norma, now, come on. That's enough, now!' I shouted, astonished that a woman in her condition could have got from one side of the pub to the other so quickly.

When I did finally get her to the porch and out of the door, she burst into tears, so I ended up consoling her.

'You really have your work cut out here, don't you, Chris?' Billy commented, as a fact rather than a question, when I finally rejoined him. He could not believe how so much could be going on in a pub on a Monday evening. There were also three other incidents that night.

Ged and Richard had been good mates for years, although they often behaved like a married couple, squabbling and sometimes not talking to each other. One occasion on which they fell out was at the time of Ged's sixtieth birthday. His wife had called Richard and told him that she was organising a surprise party for him at our pub, so could he let everyone know? However, not only did Richard not turn up, but he also failed to let anyone else know.

'I couldn't get the time off. Anyway, work comes first,' Richard shouted in his defence when asked by Malcolm why he had not turned up.

'Well, why didn't you let anyone else know?'

'Because his wife told me it was a surprise party!' he protested.

'But, Richard, you've still got to let people know. It was only Ged you had to keep it from!' Kirpal chimed in.

Richard had some of the most recognisable catchphrases in the pub. 'That's by the bye,' was a favourite of his when he was dismissing somebody else's point of view. 'I'm gobsmacked!' he would exclaim at something that did not appear that surprising to anyone else. However, his favourite was 'With all due respect...' with which he would always begin a sentence when somebody had annoyed him.

One occasion on which Richard really blew his top was when Ivor brought him in some rhubarb from his garden and it disappeared. He certainly did not react in the way that Ged usually did; he went berserk, bashing an ashtray on the bar. The following evening, Ralph, Scottish Dave and Nick got their money's worth out of it by bombarding General with questions about Richard's outburst.

'I wish I'd been here to see it,' they said, one after another. This was an example of how the regulars thrived on any gossip or even the smallest scandal in the pub.

To be fair to Ricardo, he would always apologise for any outbursts the next time he came in. After one occasion, when he had upset Banana, he was waiting the following morning for the pub to open with a book about cats to give to her by way of an apology.

On one occasion, there was a group of us drinking at the bar and the conversation got round to the rich American who had bought London Bridge, thinking he was buying Tower Bridge. The conversation moved on to the Routemaster that had had to leap from one bascule to the other when the bridge began to rise with the bus still on it.

'Did you 'ear about the time in the fifties when a double decker was hanging off the edge as it was being raised to let a big boat through?' Dennis asked Banana.

'You're joking.'

'He ain't; it's true, and do you know what as well?' General chimed in.

'What?'

'Ged was driving it!'

We all fell about laughing before Banana added, 'And Richard was standing there shouting, "Mind the Gap!"'

A Tale of Two Estate Agents

One of the most important parts of being a landlord is stepping in to stop trouble before it starts and also ejecting troublemakers. On some occasions, you can end up defending people twice your size if you are a small bloke, like me, or even smaller, like General (sorry, General, I know I've only got one joke!).

There was one occasion when I had to step in to protect Sandy, a great character who died of a heart attack at the age of thirty-three on Good Friday, 2002. He ran the estate agents' opposite the pub, although we did not find this out until after his death as he had always led us to believe it was his dad's business. Sandy Shaw, as we called him, was half-Indian, half-English and was an ex-public schoolboy who, despite being very wealthy, sometimes had holes in his shoes. Mind you, unlike the original Sandie Shaw, at least he had something on his feet! He used to come out with classic one-liners, and he always called me 'Young Chris' and Scouse Steve 'Young Steve'. He said we were the only ones worthy of this title! He once called Stuart the barman 'Young Stuart', but he told him that it was only on an occasional basis after Stuart got a bit overexcited.

Sandy used to drink very heavily and would usually buy two Mars bars and a Twix to take home with him. If he did not, then he would invariably visit the fast food place opposite and demolish a large takeaway. Therefore, what happened to Sandy in the end was not a massive surprise, but it was very sad.

He was a nervous person who would only converse or mix with people he felt totally comfortable with. One Friday evening, there was a Scotsman with a limp in the Duke who was trying to befriend Sandy. I do not think he was batting for the other side; he just wanted to talk to him. Every time he approached him, Sandy would move away, not subtly but in a dramatic fashion. I am sure the man had no untoward intentions, but Sandy certainly felt threatened. After about the fourth time of moving away, Sandy came up to me.

'Chris, help me! I'm being stalked!'

I wanted to burst out laughing, but realised that he was seriously worried by this stranger. At that moment, the man approached him again.

'Look, mate, leave him alone now.'

'Why?'

'Because he just wants to be on his own,' I explained.

'But I just want to talk to him; he's a nice guy,' he enthused.

'He doesn't want to talk to anyone,' I insisted.

'Can I buy him a drink, then?' he persisted. He turned round and asked Sandy, 'Excuse me, what are you drinking?'

It reminded me of the scene in *Fawlty Towers* in which the chef gets drunk and persistently tries to force his affections on Manuel!

'Look, this is your last chance; if you don't leave him alone, you'll have to leave,' I warned him.

'OK, I'll leave him,' he reluctantly agreed.

However, within minutes, he was pestering Sandy again, so I had to go over and ask him to leave. I felt a bit sorry for him, as I do not think he meant any harm, but I had to do it. He was still in the Hounslow area when we left the pub; I used to see him limping about.

Sandy was not the only estate agent who frequented the pub. Alan, who ran the estate agents' next door to Sandy's, also drank in the pub, although he did not become a regular until after Sandy's death.

Although Alan was bright and well-educated (he had had a private education in Uganda before Idi Amin expelled all the Asians), he could be a real know-all. He would start shooting his mouth off after a few drinks and sometimes be really rude to people. However, on several occasions, he was put in his place by Kirpal when he started bringing up various historical issues. Thereafter, he always behaved better when Kirpal was in the pub. It was the same with 'Donegal Dave', who also appeared to be overawed by Kirpal's vastly superior knowledge. I must stress, though, that Kirpal would only ever bring the loudmouths or arrogant people down a peg or two.

Alan was obviously not his real name, as, as I have already mentioned, he was an African Asian. He did have a black grandmother, but he would get very angry if anyone ever described him as 'black' within his ear range. In fact, he seemed to have a real complex about it and would insist that he was an 'African Asian'.

On the plus side, I do have to say that Alan was often very generous and on a few occasions bought everyone in the pub a drink.

On one occasion, he was pressurising our barmaid Michelle to go out with him.

'No, thanks, Alan,' she replied.

'Come on, Michelle. Just for a drink, nothing else,' Alan continued.

'No, Alan, I don't want to!' Michelle replied, more firmly.

'Michelle, come on. I'm not taking no for an answer!' he persisted.

'Well, you're going to have to, because I'm not going out with you ever!' insisted Michelle.

'I'll speak to Chris, then,' he warned her.

'You can speak to Chris, then, but it won't make any difference whatsoever!'

I was drinking at the bar nearby and had been eavesdropping, so I had heard every word of the conversation.

'Chris, I have asked Michelle out for a drink. That is all I want, nothing more, and she will not accept!' Alan told me indignantly.

'Well, that's her choice, Alan,' I retorted.

'Can't you persuade her?' he asked.

'Of course I can't!' I replied. 'I wouldn't even try to, as it's up to her what she does.'

'You're her boss, aren't you?' he protested.

'I am in here, but not outside!' I answered in disbelief.

'Well, if you don't, you won't ever see me in here again!' he announced.

'That's up to you, Alan,' I responded, becoming increasingly irritated by his pettiness. 'How would you feel if I came into your office to buy a house and told you I wouldn't buy it unless your secretary would come out with me for the night?'

'I would make her go,' he insisted.

'What if she didn't want to go?'

'I would make her go,' he repeated.

'What a load of bollocks!' I replied disbelievingly.

He eventually stormed out in a fierce temper, only to return the next evening, claiming that we had been really rude to him!

About a month later, he was propping up the bar, having a drink, when he started telling me about a two-bedroom property in St Stephen's Road that was for sale. This was the nicest road in Hounslow and he told me he could let me have it at a bargain price.

'What sort of bargain price?'

'£160,000 for you!' he replied.

'You're joking; that's a great price!' I enthused.

'Well, if you are interested, come over tomorrow and I'll take you round there to have a look,' he offered.

The next morning, I went over to the estate agents', where he was alone. That was a shame, as I might have insisted on taking his secretary out!

'I can't come with you, as I'm very busy,' he announced. 'But you can have the keys and go round and have a look at it,' he added, much to my surprise, as I was certain that this was not the usual procedure.

He reached up to retrieve a file from the shelf before opening it and showing me a photo. 'This is the place,' he said.

'That's not St Stephen's Road,' I protested, noticing the bus stop situated outside the block of flats. St Stephen's Road is a beautiful tree-lined road with lovely buildings, whereas this block looked very ordinary.

'Don't worry; the flat is at the back of this block and backs onto St Stephen's Road,' Alan assured me as he handed me a set of keys.

I was rather dubious, but decided to go round and investigate. I drove to the block of flats I had seen in the photo and parked round the back. Alan had told me that it was number thirty-seven and that was what was written on the tag attached to the keys, but these flats only went up to number twenty-four.

'Very strange,' I mumbled to myself as I called Alan on my mobile.

'Alan, I'm at the flats now, but there isn't a number thirty-seven here…' I started to explain.

'I told you to go round the back!' he yelled at me before slamming down the phone.

'The fuckin' cheeky bastard!' I shouted as I jumped into my car. I was fuming as I headed back to his office to confront the rude bastard. I got to a set of traffic lights about five minutes away when some doubts started creeping in.

Maybe I had a brainstorm and went to the wrong place, I was thinking.

'Come on, Chris. This is too good an opportunity to miss out on,' I said, trying to convince myself.

I turned the car round and drove back, only to go through the same thing all over again. However, this time I waited for somebody to come out of the block so that I could go in and have a look around, but of course there was still no number thirty-seven.

'The bastard's fuckin' winding me up!' I shouted on the way back to the pub.

By about 5.15 p.m., I had calmed down sufficiently to take the keys back and had also decided how to play the situation.

'Here are the keys, Alan. Thanks a lot!' I shouted cheerily as I placed them on his desk.

Alan looked stunned. That certainly was not the reaction he had expected from me.

'W-what did you think of it, then?' he stuttered.

'It's not too bad, but not really my cup of tea,' I told him, enjoying the puzzled expression on his face.

'Oh, really; w-why's that then?' he asked.

'I'll tell you later; I'm really busy now!' I called out, closing the door behind me.

The next day, Alan came into the pub and was as friendly as anything. I could tell that he was dying for me to mention the previous day. I talked about the weather, football, the price of half a dozen eggs, anything but property. He could no longer contain himself.

'So, what did you think of the apartment, then?' he enquired.

'Oh, it's an apartment now!' I smiled to myself. 'Like I told you yesterday, it's OK, but it's not really what I'm looking for.'

He looked at me in astonishment, as he had no doubt expected me to tell him how I had been on a wild goose chase and so on.

'Wasn't it where you expected?' he probed.

'Oh, no, it's not because of anything like that. I'm just not interested.'

I could tell that he was totally baffled. Over the previous couple of years, I had seen how he behaved and had come to realise that he was a very strange bloke who thrived on belittling people. Sometimes even the way he bought drinks for people seemed to be making a comment like, 'I've got more money than you, so I can afford it.'

Over the course of the next few months, he became more and more obnoxious until we eventually ended up barring him. Not too long after that, he was drinking in a pub called Shannons, which was located only two minutes away from us, with a business partner. By all accounts, he had had plenty to drink by the time they left to go back to the office that their cars were parked outside. The partner got into his car, while Alan went into the office to collect something. He locked the shop, climbed into the driver's seat of his car, started the engine and drove straight into his partner's car. Alan reversed up so that the shocked man could inspect the damage, but, while he was assessing it, Alan's car vaulted forward, crushing his partner between the two cars, killing him in the process. Alan, I believe, got sentenced to three years for killing the married father of two. What justice did his family get? Especially considering the fact that many people who knew him were extremely sceptical of whether it was an accident or not. I suppose it was just another case of an estate agent getting away with murder.

'Maybe he was luring you to a flat so he could kill you!' Banana suggested in reference to the time when he had had me looking for a flat that did not appear to exist.

'Yeah, you could be right there!' I agreed.

'Absolutely shocking,' commented Father Peter, our eccentric Jesuit. 'I would have sentenced him to a minimum of ten years, and he would have had to serve the full sentence,' he added.

'I thought God preached forgiveness, Father Peter,' remarked Richard, who was in one of his sarcastic moods.

'Why, of course the Good Lord does, Richard, and I am sure

he will forgive me for saying that that man deserved at least ten years!' was Father Peter's response. Even Richard had no reply to that!

Ivor the Terrible

Ivor, the man who provided the rhubarb when Ricardo had his one-man rampage, was a really good regular customer for us. When we first took over the pub, he only used to come in on Saturdays and drink Kaliber, as he was on medication. He had his neck in a collar and was on crutches as a result of an accident he had had at work when he plummeted from the eighth floor (about ninety feet) and only survived through landing in a skip, which broke his fall.

'I wish I'd been there,' shouted Gurmit. 'Then I could have moved that fucking skip!' he added, on one particular occasion when Ivor was driving him mad.

Ivor never talked but always shouted, and he would announce every regular's arrival in the pub by yelling at the top of his voice: 'Hello, Roland! Hello, Mark!' or whoever happened to be entering the pub.

'I'm sure somebody pushed Ivor off that building,' somebody like Scottish Dave or Big Mark would comment when Ivor was being particularly maddening.

Ivor was a Ronnie Corbett lookalike who thought he was a stud! A lot of it started when he would do this funny dancing, which usually ended with him doing a head-over-heels on the dance floor. Banana, Cath, June, Alison, Faye, Fiona and some other girls would muck about and flirt with him. The trouble was that he would take it seriously, really believing that they fancied him!

Ivor travelled to Thailand, where his 'girlfriend' was from, twice a year. However, having a girlfriend did not stop him travelling to Salisbury to meet a businesswoman he had met on the Internet. He claimed she paid him £150 to have sex in a hotel room, which she also paid for. He would disappear for a few days at a time, telling us that he was away 'working'.

The Thursday after one of Ivor's 'working' trips, Deaf Ivor

came into the pub. It may not sound nice referring to him as 'Deaf Ivor', but there were two Ivors who drank in the pub and this was the only way we could distinguish between the two when discussing them. It was the same as a football team I once played for when we had two Johns, one black and one white. We always referred to the black one as 'Black John' (where are my records, by the way, John?). Mind you, we had our doubts about how deaf 'Deaf Ivor' actually was on the occasion when he came back into the main bar after going to the toilet and asked, 'Whose dog is that barking out the back?'

'I saw one of your regulars drinking in the Moon on the Square in Feltham today,' he announced. People would always get a thrill out of telling us that they had spotted one of our regulars in another pub.

'What regular? I asked, not really that concerned about who it was.

'The other Ivor!' he shouted.

I did not give it another thought even two days later, when the other Ivor ('Ronnie Corbett') entered the pub with a big grin on his face.

'Hello, Ivor. I haven't seen you for a few days,' I commented.

'Well, you wouldn't have done, because I've been working,' he shouted excitedly. I was quite surprised, as I knew he had not worked since his fall five years previously.

'Really? What have you been doing, then?' asked Nick.

'I'm an escort. The businesswoman I serviced in Salisbury told her two sisters how good I was, so I've been there, working with those two. I've only just got back,' he added.

Habba, Richard, Ged and Livi were all greeted as they entered the pub by Ivor shouting their name and following it up with, 'I've been working. She paid me £180, as it was for eight hours instead of the six I was "on the job" with her sister,' he explained modestly.

'I've got a new job as an escort!' he announced to Steve and Harry as they came through the door for their usual after-work pint.

'You're not an escort; you are actually a male prostitute,' pointed out Scottish Dave.

'That's true, I'm a male prostitute!' Ivor shouted with even greater enthusiasm. From that moment on, everybody who entered the pub was greeted by Ivor announcing 'I'm a male prostitute' to them before they had even reached the bar.

'I've had my spies out on you, drinking in other pubs,' I remarked to Ivor later that evening.

'Where?' he asked abruptly.

'In the Moon on the Square in Feltham.'

'I haven't been there for ages,' he claimed, completely on the defensive. 'Anyway, who told you; Deaf Ivor?'

'Yeah, it was, actually. He told me he saw you in there yesterday.'

'I saw him in there ages ago!' he shouted.

'Don't worry about it, Ivor; I'm not that bothered,' I said, smiling. I was a bit taken aback at how angry he had got. It was only later that it occurred to me that, if he had been in the Moon On The Square in Feltham the previous day, then he had not been in Salisbury, as he claimed, and, not surprisingly, that meant that the whole male escort/male prostitute story was a figment of his imagination. I only told General, Gurmit and Malcolm, and we all agreed to play along with it, as he was not doing any harm and it was good entertainment value.

The two Ivors once clashed on a pub beano to Calais. Deaf Ivor had been a real pain all day. He was very tight generally and spent the entire day scrounging drinks off everybody. He also stole a euro off the pool table and then accused General of fiddling the whip that we had eventually organised, as it was obvious that a tight bastard like him was never going to get a round in. We started winding up the other Ivor, who we were calling 'Ivor the Engine', as he could go on for eight hours! Mind you, he could talk for longer than that.

'Deaf Ivor's been having a go about you.' General told him.

'What's he been saying?'

'He said that there's only room for one Ivor on this trip.'

'You're joking,' responded the ever-gullible Ivor the Engine.

'He told me he's gonna do you with his walking stick,' I added. This was going to be interesting, as they both had walking sticks!

'Oi, what have you been saying about me, then?' Ivor the Engine shouted at Deaf Ivor as he came out of the bar and walked over to where we were sitting outside.

'What do you mean?' asked a startled Deaf Ivor.

'You heard me. I hear you've been slagging me off!' shouted Ivor the Engine, poking Deaf Ivor in the chest.

'You're talking rubbish. I haven't said anything about you,' responded Deaf Ivor shoving the other in the chest.

After pushing and shoving each other for a few moments, they both picked up their walking sticks and proceeded to have what looked like a swordfight! It was hilarious, watching this and also seeing the looks of amazement they were getting from the locals. Both of them were small, both had dark hair, both wore glasses, both had walking sticks, both were behaving like hooligans and, of course, both were called Ivor. There was one big difference between them both, though, and that was that Ivor the Engine was, on the whole, sociable and often great fun. He was also very generous and helped everyone out on numerous occasions.

One Thursday night, I rang the bell and went to put the till in the safe. When I came back down, I noticed that the bar flap was up. I looked suspiciously at Ivor and the nutty girl he was drinking with and spotted that their glasses were once again full.

'Chris, can you let us out, please?'

I grabbed the keys and went to let two regulars out.

'By the way, watch that girl and Ivor, as they just went behind the bar and topped their drinks up,' one of them warned me.

'It's OK, I know,' I replied.

After locking the door, I marched over to the guilty two and snatched their drinks from the bar.

'Hey, what are you doing?' the dodgy girl demanded to know.

'Well, seeing as you helped yourselves to these drinks, I'm tipping them down the sink,' I explained.

'Oh, shit, you caught us, then,' she commented, pretending to be embarrassed, although I could tell that she was not in the least bit bothered.

'Right, out you go, then,' I insisted as I ushered them to the exit.

'We were only having a bit of fun,' she said, smirking, as she obviously got a buzz out of this sort of thing. Meanwhile, Ivor had not said a word and seemed to be in complete shock.

I opened the door to let them out.

'You shouldn't be so uptight,' was the advice she offered me.

Fuck off, you stupid bitch! was what I felt like saying, but instead I found the words 'Don't bother coming back' coming out of my mouth.

'Chris, I'm really sorry,' mumbled Ivor.

'What do you mean you're sorry? I trusted you.'

'I know. I'm really sorry,' he repeated.

'You know what you did is stealing,' I scolded him. 'You did it to impress that stupid cow, didn't you?'

'Not really... I...' Ivor stammered.

'You know she couldn't give a toss about you, don't you?' I continued. 'She walked out of here laughing. It's all one big joke to her, but it's your local.'

'Chris, I'm...'

'Oh, just go home. I'll speak to you tomorrow,' I told him impatiently.

The next day, I was behind the bar when in waltzed the dodgy girl from the previous night. She strutted up to the bar, as bold as brass.

'A pint of Kronenbourg.'

'You are joking?' I asked her.

'No; a pint of Kronenbourg, please,' she repeated.

'Have you forgotten what you did last night?' I asked her.

'We were only having a laugh,' she said.

'Only having a laugh? Go on, clear off.'

'Don't you think you're going a bit over the top?' she asked.

'OK, I'll tell you what. If you want me to go over the top, I'll call the police right now and show them the CCTV recording of it. Do you want me to do that?'

'No,' she answered meekly, not knowing that I had no intention of carrying out that particular threat.

'Well, you had better go, then, and don't bother coming back.'

She turned and walked out of the pub for what I assumed would be the last time.

A few months later, Chelsea and Liverpool had just drawn 0–0 in the Champions League Semi-Final first leg. Everyone had had plenty to drink and there was a complete mix of Chelsea and Liverpool in the pub. There were never any problems, as everyone got on well. Apart from Steve and Harry, there was also James, whose old man was a Scouser, his nephew, Dave, and a few other mates, who were all Liverpool fans. There were Neilson, General, Bucket, Rob, Malcolm, Mick Denyer, Tony and Robbie Coombes and a few other Chelsea there, so there was plenty of banter going on. After hours, as I was letting someone out, I noticed this attractive blonde bird (beer goggles, perhaps) walking past, looking at me. I smiled at her and was surprised when she smiled back at me. I signalled for her to come over to the door.

'How are you?'

'I'm fine thanks. I don't suppose there's any chance of me getting in, is there?' she added hesitantly.

'Of course you can,' I replied, opening the door wider to let her in. We went up to the bar and had a quick chat. I'd had plenty to drink and quite fancied her at that moment.

'Do you want a drink?'

'Are you sure?' she asked.

'Of course I am,' I responded, thinking that this girl was a bit strange.

'Let's sit at that table over there,' she suggested. We picked up our drinks, took them over to the table she had pointed to and sat down. She took a mouthful of her drink and then smiled at me, saying, 'I didn't expect you to let me in.'

'Why's that, then?'

'Because you threw me out last time I was in here,' she claimed.

'What for?' I asked in surprise.

'For flicking my cigarette ash on the floor,' she explained.

I knew that that was not true, as I had never thrown a girl out for that reason. It suddenly dawned on me who she was. She had bleached her hair blonde and had had it cut.

'You're the girl who went behind the bar to help yourself to a drink,' I announced. 'Right, come on, you've got to leave,' I added.

'B-but you've just bought me a drink,' she stammered.

'Never mind that; you've got to go now!' I insisted. I marched her to the door opened it up and out she went.

'You're fuckin' madder than me!' she yelled as I locked the door.

There was one occasion in 2005 when Liverpool and Chelsea were playing a league match at Anfield, which finished 4–1 to Chelsea, when it was far from peaceful in the pub. In fact, it was a mini riot. Harry was getting wound up, as he always did any time Liverpool were losing, although nobody in the Duke minded, as everyone was mates with him.

However, there was a group of Albanians in there, supporting Chelsea, and one of them in particular was winding Harry up. Each time Chelsea scored, he ran up to the table where the telly was standing and started banging it vigorously. After the fourth time, Harry had had enough.

'Oi, you fuckin' dickhead, stop fuckin' doing that!'

'Fuck off,' shouted the Albanian.

'I'm telling you, fuckin' sit down and shut the fuck up!' warned Harry.

The group of Albanians all stood up and looked round. Suddenly, one of them threw a pint glass at Harry, which fortunately missed. They then followed this up by turning tables over. If they expected the backup of the Chelsea fans in the pub, they had totally miscalculated, because, as I mentioned earlier, everyone was mates, regardless of who anyone supported. Suddenly, everyone else, led by Harry, Big Mark and Malcolm, charged at them, which caused the Albanians to have a change of heart. They turned and fled out of the door like a shot. However, one of them totally misjudged the way out and ended up in the corner. He had to make an instantaneous decision. Should he turn back round and go towards the exit, where he would certainly bump into Harry and co., or escape through the window? He chose the latter option and dived head-first through it, while everyone looked on in amazement. He landed on the pavement three feet below and then got to his feet and ran off up the road, after his mates.

We went outside, where General swept up the glass and immediately noticed blood all down the wall below the broken window and a trail of it on the pavement leading up to the high street. Scouse Steve boarded up the window before we sat playing poker, waiting to see if they would return. They did not come back that night or any other night.

A Shocking Kiss

Another character in the pub was Alan: larger than life and good fun, but totally unreliable. He could sing Louis Armstrong songs as well as Louis himself! Everyone called him 'Gypsy Alan', although he was a cockney, former squaddie, so I don't know how he got that name. He reminded me of Frankie Abbott from *Please Sir!*

One evening, after hours, Alan was sitting on a bar stool at one of the big, round tables, chatting to Ged, Habba, General and myself. Habba was a popular, sociable, Ethiopian Christian who had been good mates with Bob Marley. In fact, any time I played Bob Marley, Habba would leap out of his seat and be up dancing away with his mate Livi. Anyway, on this particular night, we were having a bit of a laugh when, out of the blue, Ged leant forward and kissed Alan on the lips.

'Ugh, Ged, that's disgusting!' General, Habba and I scolded. 'That's made me feel sick,' General added.

'It was only a bit of fun,' Ged replied, trying to defend the indefensible. Alan appeared to be in a trance.

'It's not a bit of fun, Ged. It's disgusting,' we continued.

Suddenly, Alan came out of his trance.

'You fuckin' bastard. You ever do that again and you'll go right through that window!' he screamed at the frightened Ged. 'I fuckin' mean it, you bastard!'

'All right, Al, leave it,' we pleaded, although we knew that his outburst was totally justified.

'You are totally out of order. I've a good mind to knock you out for what you just did!'

'OK, Alan, calm down now,' Habba joined in, with a bit more urgency, as it looked like Alan was about to explode. Although Ged could be a real pain at times, nobody in the pub would ever have wanted to see him get hurt.

'No!' Alan shouted in an even louder voice. 'That bastard has to realise that nobody does that to me, I repeat, nobody does that to me and gets away with it. Nobody except for…'

We waited for Alan to say who the exception was, assuming it would be his girlfriend, but instead he continued:

'…my cousin, Bob!'

We all looked around at each other before falling about laughing. It was one of the funniest things I had ever heard, and looking at the expression on his face made it even funnier. He seemed bewildered as to why we were all laughing.

'Your cousin Bob?'

'Yeah, that's right: my cousin Bob, and only him.'

What made it even worse was that Bob was not Alan's cousin, but was actually his cousin's husband. Keep it in the family, eh, Alan?

With regards to Bob, he was a really good, friendly bloke who used to come in regularly with his wife, Billie. On one occasion they brought their pet macaw in with them, which was well-behaved, sitting on Billie's shoulder, until it suddenly attacked Banana, biting her on the cheek. I suppose, with a name like that, we should not have been surprised.

On another occasion, Alan, who, like Scottish John, had thirteen kids, was sitting at the table, talking to my mum and Aunty Joan. General and I were also sitting there when the conversation got round to Alan's kids.

'Can you remember when all their birthdays are?' asked my mum.

'Yeah, I can,' Alan replied, not very convincingly.

'Can you name them all?' Aunty Joan asked mischievously.

'Yeah, of course I can.'

'Go on, then, name them,' shouted my mum and aunt together.

'There's Peter, John, Christopher, Mark, David, Susan, Katie, Jackie… er… Christopher…'

'You've already said Christopher,' we shouted in unison.

'Yeah, I've got two Christophers,' Alan explained. You must have run out of names, Alan!

Alan's best mate in the pub was a bloke called Eddie, a guitar-playing Eric Clapton lookalike. Eddie always spoke with a very husky voice. Tragically, a couple of years later, he died of throat cancer, so it was probably already there.

Alan and I went to Eddie's funeral with some of the other regulars, and afterwards, as is the norm, we went back to the Cambridge to have a few drinks in his memory.

'Are you off the Guinness, Al?' I enquired, noticing that Alan was on lager, which was unusual.

'I'm on the Fosters for Eddie!' he exclaimed, in his usual over-enthusiastic way.

'But Eddie always drank Carlsberg,' I pointed out, unable to believe that he had not even noticed what his best mate had been drinking all those years.

'Oh shit, get me a Carlsberg!' Alan shouted, pushing his Fosters away as we all fell about laughing.

By far the funniest story to witness involving Alan was one night during a late drink at the pub. There were several of us there, including General, Banana, Duncan, Steve B., Dave, Kirpal and Alan. Kirpal was an old classmate of mine and was the only former pupil from our school's history to go on to graduate from Cambridge (that's the university not our pub!). He taught classical military history. He was an absolute expert on all periods of history, as it was not only his job, but his obsession. We all learnt so much from him, and, whenever he was in the pub there would always be a lively debate taking place. On one occasion, Steve Barratt was discussing history and current affairs with Kirpal and Steve was speculating about the possibility of war between Britain and other countries in the future. Kirpal's response was, 'Bring them on! Bring them on!', while gesturing with his hands, as if he were offering them out himself. Dave was known as 'Donegal Dave' and had a speaking voice like Reverend Paisley. He also made Hitler seem like Mother Teresa.

On this particular night, Kirpal was tying Dave in knots during a debate about Irish history, as Dave could only ever see it from one side. Suddenly, Dave interrupted the discussion by shouting, at the top of his voice, 'Hey, you stop that shit right now!'

We looked around to see who he was shouting at, as there was no way he would yell at Kirpal like that. Nobody would, as everybody had too much respect for him and his all-round knowledge. We realised it was Alan he was shouting at, as he had spotted him breathing from a carrier bag and had assumed that he was glue-sniffing, something I had never witnessed in any pub. Dave charged like a bull at Alan, snatched the plastic bag away from Alan's face and threw it across the floor as we all stood watching in amazement.

It went deadly silent before General shouted, 'But, Dave, I gave him the bag as he's in the middle of an asthma attack.'

We all looked at Alan and, even though it was really dark in the pub, we could plainly see that he was going a bright purple in the face. We started to panic, only to hear Dave shouting, 'Oh, Jesus Christ; oh my Lord, what have I done to him?' as he dropped to his hands and knees to frantically search for the bag he had thrown across the floor only a few seconds before.

Through a combination of too much drink, the pub being in darkness (for obvious reasons) and sheer panic, it took us what seemed like ages to find it.

'I've got it! I've got it!' yelled Dave triumphantly. He charged at Alan again, this time to ram the bag with full force onto Alan's face, knocking him off his stool. Still, Dave would not let go and Alan was going an even deeper purple due to Dave's giant hands holding the torn bag onto his face! We eventually managed to calm Dave down and found Alan a plastic bag that was not torn. It was impossible not to find the entire situation funny and, within a few seconds, we were all falling about laughing, with the exception of Dave, who was still in shock, and Alan, who was still recovering from the asthma attack and the more lethal 'attack' by Dave! To be fair to them, they both saw the funny side of it once they had recovered from the shock of Alan almost dying and Dave almost killing him!

Dave was eventually barred after General spotted him and another bloke, Kevin, leaning over and topping up their beers on the CCTV screen. In the ensuing fight, Kevin ended up getting his ribs broken by Scottish John and responded by coming back and smashing a window during the night. Kevin's dad, Pat, was an old Irishman and a real gentleman and used to drink in the pub, but he never mentioned anything.

About three years later, I was alone in the pub, clearing up, when there was a continuous knock at the door. I went to have a look and there was Kevin standing outside, gesturing for me to go outside. I unlocked the door and went outside, but instantly realised that he was not there for trouble.

'Chris, I was passing by and just wanted to say that I'm really sorry for what happened before. I was out of order, as you and General were always good to me.' (He must have forgotten the time General punched him through his porch window!) 'Look, this is a photo of my daughter. I'm a changed man now. I work hard and then go home to my family.'

It was impossible to be angry with him, as it was the first time that somebody had come to apologise for what they had done without wanting to be allowed back in the pub. In other words, it was a genuine apology and not one given for ulterior motives.

Gypsy Alan was not the most legendary Alan in the Cambridge, as this honour belonged to the very aptly-named Alan Stout. Alan would drink 14.5 pints of Guinness every day. He would be waiting for us to open the door at 11 a.m., when he would have his first pint, and continue downing them until 10.50 p.m., when he would take his final mouthful out of his fourteenth pint.

'Another Guinness, but make this one a half,' he would repeat, night after night. At 11.10 p.m., he would finish the half-pint, say his goodbyes and walk to the bus stop, where he would get his usual bus home.

Alice, the previous landlady, used to get Alan to run a few errands for her and reward him with a meal or a couple of pints. Mind you, on a few occasions, Alan got himself tobacco or a bottle of booze and told them to 'add it to Alice's account'. Alice would query as to why her bill was so much, particularly on one occasion at the local butcher's, as Alan had ordered several pounds of steak and had it put on Alice's bill. Unbelievably, she let him get away with it. I think, deep down, Alice found it amusing!

Alice also told me how, when rugby teams came in before going to Twickenham, Alan would act like he was the boss. He would go over to each group, welcoming them to the pub, and, when it was time to go, he would be standing there with his bunch of keys in his hand as if he were the landlord.

'Thank you for your hospitality, Guv'nor,' they would say, one after the other.

'No problem, lads. See you next time,' Alan would reply, obviously forgetting to correct them. Alice, meanwhile, would stand there, totally ignored.

Alan once told me that his doctor was amazed that he was still alive despite being on his Guinness-only diet. He never saw his kids; sometimes he would get a bit emotional and would then invariably put 'I Have a Dream' by ABBA on the jukebox about five times running. This was because his daughter had sung in the chorus with her classmates.

One night in August 2000, Alan gulped down the remainder of his half-pint of Guinness and walked out of the pub at 11.10 p.m.

'See you tomorrow,' he called out.

Half an hour later, he was dead, after suffering a massive brain haemorrhage on the bus whilst travelling home.

Whenever I hear 'I Have a Dream', I think of Alan. He was a rogue who would scrounge drinks at every opportunity and lie and cheat to benefit himself, but he was a character. At his funeral, the vicar summed him up as follows:

'He was a reliable, hard-working family man who never asked anyone for a penny.'

Everybody listened in amazement, and Alice leant forward, touched Ted the barman on the shoulder and asked, with a straight face, 'Ted, are you sure we are at the right funeral?'

Rangi Ram in the Cambridge

There were a few real Indian characters in the pub and none more so than David Singh, who, after almost forty years, still spoke broken English with a strong Indian accent and reminded me of Rangi Ram, the servant in *It Ain't Half Hot Mum*.

He wore a turban, had a bushy beard and always had a big smile on his face. The first time I met him, he shook my hand while continually saying, 'Bobby Moore, Bobby Moore.' Much to my amusement, I noticed that David would always utter this when introducing himself. He did not appear to be your average West Ham fanatic, so one day I asked him why he always said this when meeting someone.

'Chris, when I first come to England in 1966, I know no English,' he explained. 'The first thing I hear is "Bobby Moore". I keep hearing this and notice that people smile when they hear these words, so, when I meet someone, I shake their hand and say "Bobby Moore". They always smile and shake my hand!

'Then I learn a few more words like "hello", "goodbye", "please" and "thank you", but I always say them with the words "Bobby Moore". It's two years before I learn that he's a famous footballer! I thought it means "nice to meet you" or something like that!'

I would hear this story numerous times over the next few years, but it always made me chuckle. David would always use the present tense, even when describing an event that had occurred almost forty years before.

David ('Davinder' in Punjabi) was a real character and a proper nutcase! He would often dance to the music by jumping up and down whilst waving his arms around before lifting his turban on and off. On one occasion, a crowd from the pub football team was there for the Germany versus England game, when we won 5–1. David performed a crowning ceremony where each one of them had to sit on the throne (a high stool) and he would put the crown (his turban) on their head one after another!

The chat-up line he used on the ladies was always the same: 'When you smile, you light up the room like a full moon!'

Whenever we had a buffet laid on for a special occasion, David would pile his plate up as if he had not eaten for weeks. On one occasion, he charged at the table so enthusiastically he was unable to stop in time, causing him to jolt forward. He had to put his arms in front of him to stop him going over completely, but unfortunately he put them straight in the trifle! The kids all found it hilarious and were talking about it for weeks!

One Friday night, there was a mixed group of blokes and girls who were not a particularly nice crowd at a table. One of the girls went over to David and got him up for a slow dance. While she kept him occupied, her boyfriend walked over to where David had left his jacket, picked it up and took it back with him to the table where their group was congregated.

I walked over to their table and they immediately all looked up at me.

'Is that your jacket, mate?' I asked the lowlife who had taken it.

'What's it got to do with you?' he replied.

'Because it's his jacket and I'm gonna keep an eye on it for him,' I said, pointing at David.

'Well, he's coming back to a party with us,' he retorted.

'No, he ain't,' I argued, grabbing the jacket.

The bloke had the right hump as I took David's jacket back up to the bar, where I had been sitting. David came over with the girl who was leading him on. It was obviously a trap to get him back to their place so that they could rob him or possibly worse.

'Leave the bastard; he ain't coming back with us,' shouted the boyfriend.

'He is, ain't yer, darling?' she insisted, rubbing David's leg. David was oblivious to the danger he was in.

'No, he ain't; he's staying here,' I stressed firmly.

'What the fuck's it got to do with you, anyway?' her boyfriend asked menacingly. He had by now been joined by his mates from the table.

I was thinking about my next move when my thoughts were interrupted.

'Right, you, you, you and you, you're leaving now!' It was our mate Harry, who was an intimidating sight when angry, and that was why they left without a murmur of protest.

After they had gone, David reached into his jacket pocket and pulled out a huge wad of notes. There must have been about a thousand pounds there.

'What the fuck are you playing at, David? That bastard had your jacket over there just now. They would have had the lot, given half a chance. Don't ever leave it lying about with that amount of money in it,' I scolded.

'You're the boss, Mr Chris; whatever you say,' he replied, with hands clasped together and a great big grin all over his face.

'David, I'm telling you for your benefit not mine. You don't need to carry that sort of cash around with you. Thirty or forty pounds is enough.'

Amazingly, he appeared to heed this advice, as we did not see him flashing his money about any more.

It was coming up to closing time when David announced that he was going home.

'But, David, you had better be careful. They could be hanging around for you,' Harry warned him.

'I'll give you a lift home,' General offered generously. He then went to fetch David's numerous bags of shopping from behind the bar. David took his shopping from General, went out the back and jumped into the passenger seat of General's car.

'Thank you so very much, General,' David said as General pulled up outside his house. 'You save my life!' he added.

General finally persuaded David to get out of the car. As he was climbing out, General noticed that something was leaking from one of his shopping bags. Within moments, there was sugar all over the place! It took months to finally get rid of it all. I do not know how General would have explained this if he had been pulled over by the drugs squad after dropping David off!

Whenever David came into the pub after that, he would inform anybody who could be bothered to listen, 'General save my life!'

Anil had been born and bred in the Hounslow area and was from an Asian background. However, he spoke and acted as if he were from Memphis, as he absolutely idolised Elvis and even spoke like him. I thought that Richard was bad enough over Shania Twain, but Anil would put one record after another by Elvis on the jukebox all day long. He was a real character, though, who made us laugh.

There was another Indian bloke of about fifty, who would come in about once a week and drink double vodka chasers with his pints. He was known as 'AB' and to my knowledge he was a cab driver, although I am sure that it must have taken more than a week to get the amount of alcohol he would drink out of his system.

'Kissy kissy aye aye aye aye.' He was always shouting out this chorus from 'Lady Marmalade' and would repeat it a hundred times a night, even though it should have been 'Gitchi Gitchi ya ya da da'.

One night, Scottish Richard, who worked on the Underground, was having a discussion with Resham, a bus driver, at the bar. AB spotted them, got really excited and started yelling across the pub at them, 'One underground, one over ground,' before going into uncontrollable fits of laughter. He then repeated the scenario all over again. It was really funny, although Richard and Resham did not seem to find it amusing.

General and I suddenly realised that David and AB had never been in the pub at the same time. On a few occasions, they had literally missed each other by moments.

'They could be the same person!' General remarked.

Nothing could have surprised us any more, but David wore a turban, had a thick beard and was quite stocky, whereas AB was on the small side and clean-cut. Eventually, they were in the pub at the same time, which put paid to General's suspicions. It was like a scene from *Mind Your Language* where the Indian and Pakistani continuously argued! Our money had been on David to be the maddest in the pub, as he usually was, but we had to admit that AB was madder than him that night: a win on points, rather than a straight knock-out!

Another mad Indian was Gordon, a little bloke from Goa. He lost the plot after his marriage broke up, but there was no doubt that he loved his kids.

He had some really entertaining phrases; for example, when someone said, 'All right, Gordon' as a greeting not a question, he would reply at the top of his voice in a strong Indian accent. 'When you're all right, I'm all right; when you're not all right, I'm never all right!'

After a while, he started to add to the end of this phrase, '...and that's why your name is Chris' or whatever the name was of the person he was talking to.

Liverpool James loved all this. He would shout out 'All right, Gordon!' about five times a night just to start him off and would then out-shout him, finishing off with, '...and that's why your name is Gordon the Gopher!'

Gordon's behaviour gradually became weirder and weirder. It got to the stage at which he would dance with the fruit machine and talk to the flowers. He would put his finger against any nearby girl's hand and shout 'ding a ling a ling' at the top of his voice.

His next saying was to shout at everyone in the pub, 'Stop talking rubbish! You're all talking rubbish!' Admittedly, there was an element of truth in this statement! He would also stare at people with a manic look in his eyes while mumbling to himself. We eventually had to bar him, although it was done reluctantly, as we liked him and he made us laugh.

The Oldest Regulars

Amrik, better known as 'Indian Mick', was fond of telling everyone who could be bothered to listen, 'I'm the oldest regular in the pub. I've been drinking in here since 1966.'

He was also always bragging about all the properties he owned and always put on the pretence of being the perfect gentleman. However, he behaved like a right pervert towards any girl who happened to be alone in the pub.

After taking over from Alice, we continued her practice of cashing Mick's cheques for him over the bar. To be honest, it was a pain in the backside, but, as he spent most of it in the pub, we tolerated it. However, after a while, his behaviour was becoming increasingly intolerable. He had always been a pervert with the women, but he was becoming more and more obnoxious. He started drinking elsewhere during the afternoon before coming into the Cambridge drunk and, more often than not, he would begin sniping at people.

One particular occasion on which he upset everyone was when he accused Father Peter of cheating him after he had exchanged some euros for him. No matter how many times it was explained to Mick, he just would not or could not accept that he had got it wrong. Father Peter was worried that some people might believe these false allegations, but he had nothing to worry about, as everyone had witnessed the way Mick had been behaving.

Father Peter loved the rhyming nicknames like 'Tiziana Banana', 'Tony Baloney' or 'Gurmit the Hermit' and started adding some himself, such as calling General 'Mark the Spark'. One day, he added, with a little grin, 'Amrik would probably refer to me as "Peter the Cheater"!'

On another occasion, Mick picked a fight with Ged, although General described it as more like 'something out of *Come Dancing*'! Mind you, to be fair to Mick, he claimed that Ged had been poking his nose into his business, which was something Ged was certainly inclined to do.

One particular evening, he came in drunk and asked us to cash a cheque, which General refused by telling him, 'We can't, Mick. We haven't got enough cash in the till.'

He came in the following evening and made the same request, to which General gave the same reply.

'I have been drinking in this pub since 1966 and, when I want a cheque cashed, I expect it to be done!' he ranted.

'You may have been drinking in here since 1966, but just lately you've hardly been drinking in here at all,' General reminded him.

'If you don't cash this cheque, I won't come in here any more,' he threatened.

'Well, that's up to you, Mick, but I've already told you we're not cashing that cheque for you.'

'Right, in that case, you won't ever see me in here again,' Mick insisted.

Every evening after that, we would notice Mick peering through the window, watching what was going on. About six months later, his brother came in the pub.

'Where's Indian Mick?' he enquired.

'He hasn't drunk in here for six months,' General explained.

'Are you sure?' asked his brother disbelievingly.

'Of course I am,' replied a bemused General.

'That's very strange. I spoke to him yesterday and he told me that he's drinking in here every day as usual.'

Just a memory lapse, was it, Mick?

Despite what Mick claimed, Livi, short for Livingstone, became the longest-serving regular in the pub after old Tommy died. He had been drinking in the pub since December 1963, when the inspector from Hounslow Bus Station had brought him in for a drink after his first day at work.

What a night that must been!

He had a voice that really carried and even, when we were upstairs with the telly on, we still knew when Livi was in the pub. The only time he was quiet was when he was finishing somebody's crossword for them, as he was a dab hand at them. He came from Barbados and had been the first black conductor employed at Hounslow Bus Garage.

It was during the sixties that Livi first met Ivor – a schoolboy in short trousers at the time – when he used to run and catch Livi's bus to school. They met up again in the eighties after Ivor recognised Livi drinking in the Duke and they have been drinking partners ever since.

One evening in the Duke, there was this white liberal putting the world to rights and going on about racism.

'...And what about years ago, when there were signs saying "No Blacks"? How terrible...'

'Hold it right there,' ordered Livi. If the liberal had expected Livi's support in this debate, he was going to be disappointed. 'Let me tell you something right now. I actually liked it when I saw those signs.'

'How could you possibly like it—?' the man asked in disbelief.

'Hold it right there!' Livi interrupted, raising his voice and wagging his finger. 'I'll tell you why I liked it. I liked it for several reasons.'

We were all really interested in the reasons he had for liking these signs, but had to wait for what seemed like ages as he stared at the man, finger pointing.

'Firstly, it was these people's houses and, as far as I was concerned, it was completely up to them who they let into their house.'

'But—' the loudmouth attempted to interrupt.

'No buts,' Livi barked, getting into the swing of things. 'Secondly, I admired their honesty.'

'Any other reasons, Livi?' asked Kirpal, who, like the rest of us, was loving every moment of this.

'Yes. I also liked it because, when I saw a sign like that, I didn't waste time knocking on their door. I would only knock on doors where I had a chance. It was also at one of these places where there was one of these signs that I got fixed up. The man heard me asking a neighbour and came out and directed me to a place where he told me I would get fixed up.'

'But it's offensive...'

'It's not offensive to me,' insisted Livi. 'And, besides, you shouldn't tell people how to think.'

The loudmouth, politically correct activist finished his drink and left swiftly after being put in his place by Livi. Fortunately, he never came back.

Livi used to leave a tin of snuff behind the bar, and we would pass it to him every time he came in. A few of us tried it at different times, only to spend the next half an hour sneezing.

'You young boys, you can't take it. You're sneezing all over the place because you're not made of strong stuff like us old 'uns.'

One day, Gurmit and a few of the others got Livi's tin of snuff and mixed some pepper in it. We all waited with anticipation for Livi to come in after work and snort his snuff. After he was halfway through his pint of Guinness, he called out, 'Chris, be a good lad and pass my tin over.'

'Yes, of course, Livi,' I replied enthusiastically.

Livi scooped some powder up with his finger and, as soon as he started snorting, he began sneezing.

'What's wrong, Livi? Can't you take it any more?' Gurmit called out to him.

'I don't know what's... achoo! Achoo! I... achoo!'

'Are you OK, Livi?' Ricardo asked with mock concern.

'Have you got a cold, Livi,' I joined in.

'You old 'uns just haven't got it, Livi, have you?' teased Gurmit.

We told Livi after he had stopped sneezing what had caused it and he had a good laugh, but, as usual, he claimed that he had known all along what we had done!

Livi had only held the title as longest-serving regular for a couple of years, as 'Old Tommy' had previously held that honour. He had been drinking in the pub since 1936. Imagine the changes he had seen; not just in the pub or the area, but in the world. Hitler, Stalin and Mussolini were all flexing their muscles at the time he first became a regular. Even in the last couple of years before he died, he would still come into the pub with the aid of a walking frame and sink a few pints and whiskey chasers. He had been mugged in the toilets by two Somalians a year before we took over. Tom was an ex-Para who had fought in the Second World War and I am sure that, if he could have turned the clock back sixty years, the cowardly bastards would have run a mile.

A few of us from the pub went to his funeral and were amazed when we got there and only just managed to squeeze into the Crematorium Hall, where his service was held, due to the number of people there. Not bad for an old bachelor of almost ninety!

The Sikh Battalion

The vast majority of Sikhs who drank in the pub were great and got on brilliantly with the indigenous British. They joined in all the wind-ups and were very loyal. The best of the bunch were Gurmit, Kirpal, Resham, Jack (the Indian Tom Jones) and, of course, last but not least, David Singh. They also shared the same political views as most of us and had the same mentality.

Whenever 'Sing' by Travis came on the jukebox, we would sing 'Singh, Singh, Singh...!' pointing at Kirpal, Gurmit and Jack in the process, and they always loved it. In fact, Kirpal started putting it on about five times in a row and would then lead the chorus!

They also loved it when our mate Steve (Wef) Evans, an Englishman brought up in South Wales, came into the pub. He had spent three years in India and, as soon as he came back, he had opened up a corner shop and before long had three of them! They were actually off-licenses, but it made the story better by saying they were corner shops!

Although Gurmit could be a real wind-up, he was the best at calming situations down. On one occasion, my old school mate, Brendan, really lost his temper with a black bloke who kept pestering his girlfriend. The bloke would not leave her alone and kept putting his hands all over her, so Brendan grabbed him by the throat and threw him to the floor. He would have done him some serious damage, but Gurmit calmed him down. Brendan admitted afterwards that Gurmit was probably the only person in the pub who would have been able to do that.

Gurmit would really liven up after a few drinks, especially after going on the double Bacardi and Cokes. One Friday night, after plenty to drink, Gurmit arranged to take a Polish girl into Central London the next day to see the sights. He persuaded a reluctant Banana to go as well.

'You won't make it tomorrow after the amount you've drunk tonight, young Gurmit,' predicted the old and wise Livi.

'Livi, if I've said I'm going, then I'm going,' Gurmit retorted sternly. 'My word is my bond!'

The next day, Gurmit came into the café and ushered Banana over.

'Banana, do me a favour. When that Polish girl comes in, tell her I'm sorry, but I can't make it today.'

'Well, that's charming, Gurmit! And aren't you forgetting that you invited someone else? Someone who has just spent an hour getting ready!'

'Oh, sorry, Pudding. I'll take you some other time,' he said apologetically. Pudding was Gurmit's pet name for Banana.

Over the next couple of months, Banana and the rest of us gave Gurmit loads of stick for letting her down. It got to him so much that he invited her to his work's Christmas party. However, a few days before she was due to attend, and after Gurmit had sunk about ten pints of Dutch courage, he broke the news to Banana that the Christmas party had been cancelled. He whispered the news to her, as he did not want the rest of us to find out, but those hopes were instantly shattered by Banana's reaction.

'Oh, here we go! "My word is my bond" Gurmit!' she screamed out.

'What's up, Tiziana? What's Gurmit done?' Ralph called out across the bar, delighted that somebody other than himself was in trouble.

Everyone was queuing up to give Gurmit stick over it and from that time onwards, whenever Gurmit made any promises, we would react by saying, 'Oh, yes, of course, Gurmit, because your word is your bond!'

A typical Gurmit wind-up was in December 2004, when Mike Smith came with my cousin Maxine to collect the birthday presents he had received at his fiftieth party the previous night. They carried them all through from the café where we had put them, while Gurmit and the others were propping up the bar. After exchanging pleasantries, they headed for the exit.

'Maxine, you've dropped one!' Gurmit called out.

'Oh, thanks, Gurmit!' Maxine replied, taking the neatly-wrapped present from Gurmit. What she did not know was that

Gurmit had grabbed it from under the Christmas tree. It was an empty box wrapped up in Christmas paper for decorative purposes, so you can imagine the shock they had when Mike Smith opened it after getting home! I have no idea why, but everybody always called him Mike Smith instead of just Mike.

Kirpal was the only pupil from Syon to go on to Oxford or Cambridge University. Being an expert in military history, he really looked up to my dad, who was a Rear Gunner in the Fleet Air Arm on the Russian Convoys during the Second World War. He took my dad to Cambridge, where they stayed on campus for a few days and my dad was treated really well.

Ged always called addressed or referred to Kirpal as 'Prof', and he was the only person Ged would not argue with in the pub.

Kirpal would often be in deep discussion with Ken about military history while propping up the bar. They would go to museums or to places like Portsmouth for the weekend.

Steve Barrett was another regular who found Kirpal really interesting company. They had an ongoing quiz game where they would fire questions at each other on historical battles. Although Steve was very knowledgeable, I am sure he would be the first to admit that Kirpal was unbeatable.

My old football manager, Tommy Mackin, is a real character who lived for football but was also very knowledgeable about world affairs. One night, he came into the Duke for a few pints and got chatting to Gurmit.

'Are you a Sikh?' he asked Gurmit.

'Yes, of course.'

'Good lad. Up the Sikhs, up the Sikhs, up the Sikhs!' Tom began shouting at the top of his voice.

Tom has always been completely obsessed with football, especially his team the New Inn, based in Brentford – a team I played for in the early nineties. He would always be on the lookout for new talent, whether he was on the bus, in the pub or in the laundrette. On one particular occasion, Tom was in the bookies when he got chatting to a young stocky bloke putting a few bets on.

'Do you play any football, my old mate?'

'Yeah, I play a bit.'

'A centre half are you, son?'

'Yeah, that's right, I am.'

'Well, how about joining my team then. We've got a great bunch of young lads, but I've lost my centre half, so you might be able to do a job for us,' Tom enthused.

'I'd love to, but I'm already playing for someone,' the youngster explained.

'Well, who do you play for, then?' Tom demanded to know, quite perturbed that this young man could even consider declining his offer.

'Chelsea!' replied the young John Terry who, within a few years, would be Chelsea captain. Fortunately, the Chelsea chairman at the time, Ken Bates, did not hear about this or Tom could have been up before the FA for making an illegal approach!

One day, Tom asked me why my brother was known as General.

'It's his real name, Tom,' I replied.

'You're kidding. Why on Earth has he got a name like that?' he asked.

'Well, my dad was in the army, so he insisted on calling all my brothers by military names,' I explained.

'Why, what are your other brothers called, then?' Tom enquired with great curiosity.

'Well, there's Field Marshal, Lieutenant, Major, Brigadier, Colonel and then, of course, General,'

'Well, I never!' he enthused. 'But how comes you're called Chris?'

'My dad wanted to call me Private, but my mum put her foot down and insisted on calling me a normal name like Chris, as she was fed up with all her sons having militaristic names,' I explained to a fascinated Tom.

'That's absolutely brilliant!' Tom shouted, before telling everybody who was about this 'incredible story'.

A few months later, we were in the pub when my brother Steve came in.

'Tom, this is my brother, Steve,' I announced, forgetting all about my wind-up.

'Steve? Steve?' Tom repeated, with a puzzled look on his face.

'I thought all your brothers had military-type names.'

I burst out laughing, so Tom realised that I had been winding him up. He then yelled out his catchphrase.

'You murder me, Chrissy!' before adding 'I've told every bloody person I've met since that story!'

The Cat's Whiskers

One customer with whom I clashed heavily was known by everybody as 'Cat' due to his resemblance to Catweazle the wizard, who used to be on telly in the seventies. He was a complete fruitcake and this was obvious the first time he came into the pub. He roared up on his motorbike as if he were Marlon Brando in *The Wild One*, whereas, to be honest, he was more like Freddie Mercury in the 'Crazy Little Thing Called Love' video!

He was the most boring person I had ever met in my life. General and I both hated the quiet nights when one or other of us was working while Cat was propping up the bar. I would often pretend that somebody needed serving in the other bar just to get away from him. I used this tactic one boring Monday night and went into the public bar to escape from his tedious stories. The bar was completely empty, but I was chatting away so that Cat would think I was serving somebody. Suddenly, the door burst open and in walked Cat while I was in mid-sentence.

'I thought you said that you came round here to serve someone,' he said accusingly.

'I did; he's just left,' I lied, very unconvincingly.

He claimed that he lived with a girl and was in a steady relationship, but most of us found that hard to believe, as he worked every day and came straight to the pub from work. About once a week, at just before closing time, he would down his pint in one and march to the door.

'Are you off, Cat?' somebody would invariably ask him.

'Phone call,' he would announce, in the most serious voice he could put on. This was despite the fact nobody ever heard his mobile ring!

One Monday night, General was working behind the bar when somebody mentioned Brentford (the town, not the football club).

'Suicide City!' Cat yelled across the bar.

'Sorry?'

'Suicide City!' he repeated excitedly.

'You what, Cat?'

'Brentford's known as Suicide City!'

'Since when?' asked General. 'I've lived round here all my life and I've never heard it called that.'

'It has the worst record in fatalities from road accidents in the country,' Cat announced. 'One day…' Everybody started saying 'oh no' in much the same way as Rodders and Del Boy did when Uncle Albert began a sentence with 'During the war…'

'…I was on my bike, roaring through Brentford,' he continued, 'when I saw a motorcyclist crash into the side of a bus. Passers-by went to help and one started to remove the injured motorcyclist's crash helmet. I didn't have time to warn him against doing this, so I rode towards him at full speed and kicked him straight in the jaw.'

'What happened then, Cat?' asked an amused but disbelieving General.

'I had knocked him out. The paramedics turned up and didn't know which one of them to tend to first. They took them both away in an ambulance.'

'Didn't anyone say anything to you?' Scottish John asked him.

'Yes; one of the paramedics asked me why I had done it, so I asked her, "How many roadside accidents have you attended?" She said that she had no idea and asked me how many I had attended, and I told her it was 372 at the last count!'

'372! No way!' Ged shouted.

'I'm telling you, I've attended 372 roadside accidents,' Cat insisted.

This was one of his more amusing stories, as most of them were really mundane. I fell out with him not long after this and he never came back into the pub again. This did not bother me a great deal, as it meant I did not have to listen to his boring stories any more, although, having said that, I have to admit that he was certainly a character.

There was a man from the Seychelles called David, who used to play the guitar and sing some old classics while wearing a Stetson. He had a fantastic voice, which carried him through, as his guitar playing was pretty average. During the day, he would busk in Hounslow High Street, and he was eventually deported for, it was rumoured, an unhealthy interest in underage girls.

David's manager was a small Scottish bloke called Kenny, who also used to wear a cowboy hat and claimed he carried a gun when working in customs over at the airport. He was small, wore glasses and could have been Ged's Scottish double to look at. He used to be as good as gold until he got drunk, and then he could be a pain. On several occasions, I had to carry him to and then put him into a cab.

On one occasion when he had had a few too many, he strutted up to Harry, who was sitting at the table having a drink with his girlfriend Carla, looked him straight in the eyes and asked him, 'Are you ready to rock 'n' roll?'

'No, I don't dance!' replied a surprised Harry.

Kenny turned and staggered away. It was only about thirty minutes later when I had to help him to his cab, but that was after Harry had called me over.

'You see that nutter over there?'

'Who, Kenny?' I asked, smiling.

'Yeah. He just came over and asked me if I was ready to rock 'n' roll and I just said that I didn't dance,' he explained, laughing. 'It's just clicked: he wasn't asking me to dance; he was offering me out!'

Kenny had a really nice girlfriend called Kerry and they appeared to get on well apart from when he drank too much. One Saturday night, Kenny; Kerry; Deckland, a crazy Irishman; Banana; I and a couple of others were having a late drink when the conversation took a serious turn. Kenny suddenly got emotional and admitted to hitting Kerry at different times, and Kerry started crying.

'You bastard! How can you do that to this poor girl?' Banana yelled at him.

'I know. I don't know why I do it. I really love her.'

'But you are a coward, doing that to her,' Banana continued shouting.

'He says sorry and promises never to do it again, but then he does,' Kerry revealed in between sobs.

Kenny then started to explain what had made him an emotional wreck. To cut a long story short, he had come home to find his parents and sister dead. They had been murdered. We sat there in suspense, waiting to hear what happened next, as Kenny was struggling to get the words out.

It was so quiet you could have heard a pin drop when suddenly, out of the blue, Deckland interrupted the deathly silence.

'Chris, come and let me out. I can't listen to this nonsense any longer!'

Banana and I to this day still cannot believe what bad timing that was. I had known Deckland since the 1980s and knew how eccentric he was and that he often behaved in a bizarre way, such as the time he barred all the Irish from drinking in Hounslow Football Club during his time as manager there, but this was incredibly bad timing and insensitive to say the least!

Another little Scotsman who was a real character was a little chubby man of about eighty-six called James Connelly. He used to make loud squealing noises that sounded like 'Duck, duck, duck, duck, duck!' and shout across the pub even when Chris Swan was not there!

He could really knock the drinks back for someone of his age, but the problem was that he could be a bit like David Singh in flashing his money around. On one occasion, he had had a big win on the horses and, within ten minutes, everyone in the pub knew, as he was waving his winnings around in the air. There were a few people in there that night who I did not completely trust, so I told James I would give him a lift home. Bucket, a friend and a real character, was also in the pub in his usual drunken state, and, as he lived around the corner from James, I offered him a lift as well.

What a mistake that was! Two hours later, I was driving round Isleworth, as neither of them could remember where they lived.

'Do you want a bunch of fives?' James was shouting at Bucket in the back of the two-door Fiesta.

'Come on you two; I wanna get home,' I pleaded. 'We've been driving round in circles all night. If we're not careful, we'll get a pull soon.'

Just as the words had come out of my mouth, a police car pulled out of a side road and it was now right behind me. I was certain they must have been able to hear the racket James and Bucket were making in the back of the car. As expected, they signalled for me to pull over.

'Do you know why we have pulled you over?'

'No; why have you?'

'Well, we noticed that you have been driving all around here tonight. Is there any particular reason?'

I explained exactly why I had been driving around for hours and both officers listened before approaching my car to check whether I was telling the truth.

They opened the passenger door and looked into the back seat, to be greeted by Bucket singing his own version of 'We'll Keep the Blue Flag Flying High' and James Connelly shouting. 'Officers, do you want a bunch of fives?'

'Oh, no, not you two!' one of the officers remarked before slamming the door shut.

'We see what you mean,' one of them said to me in a sympathetic tone. 'Well, good luck!' they called out as they walked swiftly back to their car.

10,000 Dave Coopers, 'J Arthur' Neilson, a Bucket and a White Swan

Dave Cooper was a Father Christmas lookalike who always had a big grin on his face, but you would see him smiling the most whenever he had a pint in his hand. He is the only man I have ever seen drinking from an empty pint glass without noticing it was empty! He would frequently fall asleep standing up, but he would never let go of his pint. On the occasions when he did notice that his glass was empty, he would just pick up the nearest pint to him and start drinking that. He usually came in with his partner in crime, Cookie, who would end up just as drunk.

One particular Sunday night, Dave was in his usual drunken state as he staggered off to the toilet. After about twenty minutes, I noticed that he still had not returned, so I sent Stuart, our Scottish barman, to go and check that he was OK.

'He's OK; he's sitting on the toilet,' Stuart informed us.

Another twenty minutes had elapsed when I asked Stuart to go and check on him again.

'He's still on the toilet, but he's on the one in the other cubicle now!' Stuart said, laughing.

There was one occasion in the pub when Dave was in a session with Bucket, Neilson and Kirpal. There was an Irish bloke at the bar who started being abusive. Rab was working behind the bar, but, as usual, he was too scared to say anything. The man spent the next hour and a half insulting Dave, who just sat there, supping his beer in his usual relaxed manner. The Irishman eventually got fed up goading Dave, as it seemed obvious that he was not going to get a reaction from somebody so laid back.

'What you lookin' at, you ugly bastard?' he shouted at Bucket.

'What did you say?' asked a bemused Bucket, completely shocked that somebody could think he was ugly.

'You heard, you bastard,' the drunk repeated.

Suddenly, Dave was out of his seat as fast as lightning. He charged at the abusive man and knocked him flying off his stool. The man did not know what had hit him as he sat on the floor in a daze. Dave returned to his stool, picked up his pint and carried on as if nothing had happened.

What it boiled down to was that Dave could take endless abuse himself, but if anyone had a go at one of his friends they were in big trouble. That was the day that Kirpal made a comment that he repeated many times:

'10,000 Dave Coopers would take over the world!'

The great thing about Dave and his drinking partner, Cookie, was that no matter how drunk they were, they would always have a smile on their faces. Dave, Bucket, Neilson, Mick Denyer, Paul Carter, Swanny, Dave Dean, Tick, Tony Coombes and Dave Coombes have all been friends with General for about thirty years or more and Finnigan even longer. Dave Campbell, a 6'10" QPR fan, whose claim to fame is how he ran a mob of Dutch single-handed in Germany in 1988, is another one. Shocking behaviour!

'West Ham Sam' is another old mate, who, despite moving to Manchester, would still make the odd appearance. His eyesight was worse than 'Colonel Blink the Short-sighted Gink' who starred in Beezer. We would know when he was arriving, as we could hear all the sirens!

Bucket was always the life and soul of the party when he came into the pub. His real name is Colin, but he has been known as Bucket for years due to the fact that he would vomit after every drinking session while attending Chelsea away games. He is a small, red-headed Chelsea fanatic who is always laughing. He is like a smaller version of Ronald McDonald, although Ronald has got a better dress sense! One of his favourite tricks was to pick up a pool cue and 'play the guitar' with it to a Bowie tune.

One of the best nights ever in my time at the pub was on Scottish John's birthday in 2001. It was packed with a great atmosphere and everyone was joining in with whoever was up on the karaoke. Everyone performed well on the stage, but Bucket was the star of the show! He finished off the night with his very own version of 'Hey Jude', which went something like: 'Hey, Jude, la la la la, dah, dah, dah, dah, mmm, mmm, mmm… Come on, sing up! Sing up, you bastards, sing up! Come on, I can't hear you! Sing louder, you bastards!' until the whole place was singing as loud as possible! Even ten minutes after the song had finished, everyone was still singing in unison, 'Na na na na na na na, hey, Jude.' It was no surprise to anyone that Bucket did not know the words as he has been an ardent Chelsea supporter for over forty-five years but still does not know the words to 'Blue is the Colour'! He is the most well-known Chelsea fan in the whole area, as for years people have witnessed him staggering down the road, holding his takeaway curry, singing his own version of 'Carefree…'

Bucket, like the others I mentioned above, was a loyal Chelsea fan even when they were struggling in the old second division, so he deserved the round of applause the whole pub gave him when he marched in, waving his flag and shouting 'Champions!' after Chelsea had won the league for the first time in fifty years. He then marched straight up to Harry and yelled 'You're next' while prodding him in the chest, as Liverpool and Chelsea were due to meet in the Champions League the following week.

Swanny has been one of my best mates over the last twenty-odd years and has always been a character. He was a pre-karaoke singing star on our football tours to Hamburg, where, to the great delight of our German hosts, he would stand on the table, singing 'It Really Doesn't Matter Any More' almost as well as Buddy Holly himself.

His real name is Christopher Swan and, on one occasion he was propping up the bar with Scouse Steve when the police pulled up outside and walked towards the entrance.

'Who are they after?'

'They're coming to get you, Swanny!' joked Scouse Steve.

'Duck, Swan!' I shouted.

'You're such a wanker, Whip!' Swanny informed me. That was one of his kinder comments to me over the years.

Swanny's claim to fame was the time he ran the London Marathon and had his picture in the local paper. This resulted in numerous girls phoning him up, telling him how handsome he looked. Swanny, of course, lapped it all up, believing every word they were saying to him, not knowing that my brother Steve and I were behind it! He also conveniently forgot to mention to these girls how he had almost dropped out a few miles from the end but was coaxed, encouraged and bullied over the finish line by Steve!

One night, he turned up at the Cambridge, devastated, after some bad family news. I will not go into details, but General and I sat up and had a few drinks with him, trying to help. Rather than let him go home to an empty flat, we persuaded him to stay the night.

After a few hours' drinking, Swanny's legendary wandering eye had clocked Esther, an African woman, drinking at the other end of the bar. She had done the rounds with a few of the lads in the bar, and I am not talking about rounds of drinks. He made his move, and within about half an hour, he came bouncing over to me.

'Whip, do you mind if I take Esther upstairs?'

'On one condition, Swanny, and that is that she leaves when you do. I know what you're like!'

After about an hour, Swanny reappeared downstairs.

'Let me out, Whip.'

'No chance.'

'Come on, Whip.'

'No, Swanny, we agreed. You can't just walk out and leave her here.'

He went back upstairs like a mischievous schoolboy on his way out of the headmaster's office.

In the morning, I went downstairs and realised that Swanny had already gone. After opening the post, I went upstairs and into the end room where Swanny and his new love had spent the night.

'Cor, it stinks in here,' I commented, after opening the door to be greeted by the smell of booze, smoke and sweat. I opened the window and looked around the room. It was in a right mess. I walked up to a bundle of covers left on the floor and kicked it, only to jump back in shock as it started moaning and moving! Out from under the covers crawled Esther, totally naked! I made my excuses and left her to it!

She ended up going out with our Polish lodger, Dariusz, but drove him mad with her jealousy. He complained how she would accuse him of eyeing up the checkout girls in the supermarket when they were getting their shopping. One Saturday night in the Duke, she attacked Banana, pulling her hair because Dariusz and Banana were 'making eyes at each other'. They had, in fact, just nodded at each other across a crowded pub. Banana hit her back and Esther ran from the pub. Patricia, who was a bigger black lady than Esther, threatened to sort Esther out if she started on Banana again, as she had a really soft spot for her.

On another occasion, Swanny pulled another African girl and took her into the ladies' toilet. He has always been a romantic! After about half an hour, he reappeared just as T.Rex was blasting out of the jukebox with 'Ride a White Swan'.

'That's what she's been doing for the last half an hour,' Nielson shouted, pointing at the bemused girl: 'riding a white Swan!'

Neilson or 'Mr Neilson' as Kirpal always addressed him because, as he would stress, 'you have to show respect', was a rival for Gurmit's spot as the most popular bloke in the pub. He was always accusing everyone of having a 'J. Arthur'! In fact, he was absolutely obsessed with it. If anyone disappeared for more than a minute, he would shout, 'Don't worry; he's just gone for a good old J. Arthur!' If anybody even put their hand in their pocket for money or anything else he would immediately accuse them of 'having a crafty fiddle'.

Neilson once claimed that, when he went to see his doctor (a female) about a stomach complaint, her sound advice to him was, 'You are too full. What you need to do is go home and have a good old J. Arthur! That will solve the problem!' A doctor like that would be every bloke's dream!

Neilson's favourite hobby was to be spanked. The only condition was that it was a woman dishing out the spanking! On one occasion, we had been on a 'Jolly Boys' Outing' to Richmond, organised by 'Corporal Kirpal'. Banana came on it as well and brought back a thick, chunky tree trunk with her. She soon produced it in the pub and began threatening everyone with it. 'Mr Neilson' started pleading with her.

'Punish me with it, please! Come on; I've been a very naughty boy today!'

'No, Neilson, not you!' insisted Banana.

'Oh, why not?' the disappointed Neilson demanded to know.

'Because you enjoy it too much!' she replied.

'Oh, go on, Banana! Give him a thrashing!' chimed in the rest of us.

'OK, then, bend over, Neilson.'

Banana had not even got the words out of her mouth and yet Neilson was bending over, touching his toes, with a real look of anticipation all over his face.

'Are you ready, Neilson?' Banana asked him.

'Yes; please, hurry up!' begged Neilson.

As quick as a flash, Banana handed the thick trunk to General, who then whacked Neilson as hard as he could.

'Ugh! Ouch! Ooh, Banana! That was wonderful!'

'Do you want more, Neilson?' asked Banana.

'Yes, please!' replied the polite Neilson.

General then whacked him even harder, which prompted further squeals of delight from the sore but ecstatic Neilson. He gave him six of the best in total before quickly handing the 'offensive weapon' back to Banana.

'Cor, that really hurt!' purred Neilson. 'I didn't realise you could punish naughty boys so severely!'

'Well, let that teach you a lesson,' warned Banana.

'Same time next week?' Neilson asked, still totally unaware that the thrashing he had received had been given by General and not Banana. Sorry to break the news to you now, if you are reading this, Neilson. You know that I had nothing to do with it!

Jolly Boys' Outing to Richmond

With regards to the 'Jolly Boys' Outing', a whole crowd of us left the pub one Sunday afternoon and the first stop was to visit our barman Ted's local in St Margaret's. We had a couple of drinks with Ted and then set off to walk to Richmond. We were heading for a small pub backing onto the railway line. Kirpal had suggested going there, as he often went there for a dinnertime or after-work drink with his work colleagues at Parkshot College. Tony Baloney, who also worked in Richmond, backed him up, agreeing that it was a really good pub.

'Come on, everyone, let's get moving!' Kirpal instructed, treating the outing like a military operation.

We were messing around and it was at this stage that Banana found her punishment stick, which she kept with her not just for the rest of that day but for a couple of years after.

'Come on, Tony, keep up with me!' barked Kirpal.

Tony quickened his pace and soon caught up with Kirpal as Banana continually threatened the rest of us with the stick. We went round the bend, and Tony and Kirpal were already out of sight. Fortunately, some of us knew more or less where the pub was situated, so we found it almost immediately. However, when we entered the pub, we were surprised to see that Kirpal and Tony were not there.

'Don't worry; they'll be here in the minute,' Mr Neilson said.

We got a round of drinks in and started to relax. In fact, we were on our third or fourth pint and still there was no sign of the other two.

'Are you sure this is the right pub?' Aisha asked. She was a Scottish girl, down for a few days. She had previously worked behind the bar for us.

'Well, this is the one they described,' said General.

'Yeah, it is this one 'cause me and Banana came down here with Kirpal in the summer,' I pointed out.

'They're probably having a better time somewhere else!' remarked Gurmit.

Suddenly, the door burst open and in walked Tony and Kirpal, looking none too pleased.

'What happened to you two then?' we enquired.

'Tony got us lost!' claimed Kirpal.

'Look, don't say that. You really pissed me off back there!' Tony snarled aggressively.

'It was you who suggested going—' began Kirpal.

'Come on, boys, leave it now,' we urged, realising that the two of them appeared to be on the verge of having a punch-up. 'We'll have the inquest later to decide who's to blame.'

'What are you drinking, boys?' asked Gurmit.

Gurmit returned from the bar with their drinks and they both soon calmed down. It was not long before they were both receiving a load of stick and joining in the laughter with the rest of us.

'What we can't understand is how you both work round here and come in here with your workmates and yet you both got lost!' It was unbelievable, as both were really intelligent blokes.

'We thought we were in the wrong pub!' Aisha shouted, enjoying the banter.

Suddenly, there was a loud bang and Gurmit was lying on the floor. We all panicked, but within seconds three barmaids and a couple of other girls were surrounding him, making sure he was OK. I had also gone over there to check on him. It had been very hot and stuffy in there, and this had caused him to pass out. Tragically for poor old Gurmit, when he opened his eyes, he found himself looking straight at me! There were five lovely girls and me surrounding him, so he really got the short straw. He has never forgiven me for that! He did give us some ideas on how to attract female attention, though.

Gurmit stole the show on another occasion. It was our fourth Syon School Reunion for the boys of 1974–79, at which there were the usual suspects, with the exception of a couple of faces making their first appearance. Even Freddie Bere turned up! Sorry, Fred!

General started the ball rolling with the wind-ups.

'Chris, wind 'em up. Tell them that Gurmit went to your school as well.'

Gurmit loved a joke and a wind-up. He was chubby, wore glasses and was from an Asian background. I thought back to school and suddenly thought of someone who Gurmit could pretend to be.

'Chris, General wants to do a wind-up,' Gurmit informed me enthusiastically.

'I know he does. Listen, Gurmit: there was a chubby Asian bloke who wore glasses, called Bharatt Shah. He was in Windsor House, the same as some of them here.'

'Bharatt Shah in Windsor. OK, I've got that,' Gurmit assured me.

I gave him a few more bits of information, including some names of teachers and classmates to drop into the conversation.

I sidled up to Alan Procter and Phil Harding, who were both in Windsor, and joined in their conversation.

'Do you remember Bharatt Shah from school?' I asked them.

'Yeah; why?'

'Well, that's him sitting over there!' I pointed at Gurmit, who was propping up the bar with a big grin on his face.

'Fuck me, it is you, Bharatt! How are you, son?' Alan greeted him enthusiastically.

'I'm OK, thanks,' Bharatt c/o Gurmit replied.

'Why didn't you say "hello" earlier?' Jacko (Phil's nickname) asked him.

'I smiled and waved when you walked in, but I assumed you didn't recognise me,' Gurmit replied, with a completely straight face.

'Of course we would've done,' insisted Big Mal (Alan's nickname).

'Bharatt hasn't forgiven you two for nicking his dinner money off him at school, have you, Bharatt?' I chipped in.

'No, I haven't, and, to make things worse, I got the slipper off my dad when I got home, as he'd found out I hadn't been having school dinners!' Gurmit explained, really starting to enjoy his new role.

'Sorry about that, Bharatt,' said Big Mal.

'Yeah, I'm sorry as well,' agreed Jacko.

The evening continued, with everyone having a few more drinks and chatting away. Then Big Jack, a Tom Jones lookalike who would dance to every record of his that came on, got up to go home.

'Good night, Chris; night, General; good night, Gurmit,' he called out.

The ever-alert Big Mal's head shot round like that of the girl in *The Exorcist*.

'Gurmit? Oi, you ain't Bharatt Shah!' he exclaimed.

'We had you going, though, didn't we?' remarked Gurmit.

'Shh, Al, keep it going 'cause Jacko doesn't know yet,' I urged Big Mal, after we had finished laughing.

'Oi. Phil. What do you think of seeing old Bharatt again, then?' Big Mal asked him.

'He ain't changed a fuckin' bit, has he?' Jacko enthused. God knows how we all managed to keep a straight face.

Jacko left that night still believing that Gurmit was Bharatt Shah, a pretence Gurmit kept up at the following year's reunion. If you are reading this, Phil, it was all General's idea! If you are reading this, Bharatt, I know none of us had seen you for twenty-seven years, but you were obviously not forgotten!

'You did that well, Gurmit!' Big Mal complimented him.

'Well, it was "rent a Paki night", after all!' chuckled Gurmit.

Scottish John to the Rescue!

Scottish John, or 'John Boy' as I called him, was one of the main characters during our time at the Cambridge. John had the build of a pit bull, like a white Mike Tyson. During the first couple of years at the pub, he was in and out of work. One of his jobs was as a bus driver based at Hounslow Bus Station, next door to the pub.

After about two months, John was off sick with a sore throat. However, every day at 11 a.m. John would march through the bus station as bold as brass on his way to the pub, not caring whether he was seen.

'I've got a doctor's certificate,' he would announce to anyone who questioned what would happen if his bosses saw him drinking in the pub while off sick. By all accounts, the bosses were scared of him, and some of the other drivers would tell us about John at work. There was one occasion, a couple of weeks after he began working there, when John received a message that the General Manager wanted to see him. He went to his office, only to be told that the G.M. was too busy to see him. When John returned later to be told the same thing, he shouted, 'Right, that's twice I've been to see him. You can tell him from me that he can come and make an appointment to see me next time!'

The following year, John was working for a courier company run by a couple of brothers called Craig and Andrew. General worked there for a few months as well. One day, John clashed with Andrew, who then told Craig what had occurred. Craig went to see John.

'What was that about earlier with Andrew, then, John?'

'I'll just fight you as well, if you want,' John warned Craig.

'I don't want to fight you, John; I just want to sort the problem out,' replied a bemused Craig.

General told me that Craig thought that John was a character.

John and his wife, Helena, were a great help to us on one occasion while I was on holiday. It was a Sunday night and

General was upstairs with his three children when the barman came upstairs and said that he had to go home, as he didn't feel well.

'But I can't go down there; I've got the kids,' General explained.

'Well, I've got to go home. There are only a few people down there, anyway,' he added.

General put the kids to bed and went downstairs to be greeted by a whole group of Irish Travellers playing cards for money in the public bar, who were by now drunk and playing for high stakes. The barman had, of course, forgotten to mention this. At closing time, the Travellers still had loads of drinks that the barman had served them earlier lined up and were refusing to drink up. General had the three children upstairs, so he was in a precarious situation, especially when his youngest daughter, who was only two at the time, came downstairs in tears.

John and Helena had been just about to leave, but, on seeing the situation that General was in, changed their minds. John took his coat off again, and Helena cuddled General's daughter and took her upstairs to bed. John then went through the bar and, in his strictest Sergeant Major's voice, yelled, 'Drink up, everyone, right now, or I'm taking your glasses!'

There was no response from the Travellers, so John barked even louder.

'It's your last chance; drink up now!'

The group completely ignored John and just continued playing cards. John walked up to the biggest bloke, who looked like their leader, snatched the drink from his hand, walked over and poured it down the sink.

He marched straight back over to the table and announced, 'I'm taking the rest of these right now!'

The big bloke stood up, looked around at the others, nodded towards the door and walked out of the pub. The others all followed him without a word.

A Travelling Problem

On another occasion, we were having a birthday party for General's kids. We were all in the main bar when I suddenly noticed that there were people in the public bar, which we had closed, as it was a private party. The regulars were always invited to our private parties and always fitted in well. I walked through and saw that a group of Irish Travellers were sitting there. If you do not say anything they are straight on their mobiles and, within an hour, you have got sixty or seventy of them in your pub. I knew that this would be the case here.

'Who the fuck let them in and served them?' I asked the barman, although I already knew the answer. He was the same barman who had gone home and left General in the lurch the previous time.

'I did,' he admitted, sheepishly. 'I thought that they could drink round this bar, away from the others.'

'You stupid idiot! What's gonna happen if they start?'

He went off to hide in the corner, as usual, while I decided what to do. It was the same rowdy mob that John had got rid of. Suddenly, some women arrived to join them and I knew we had a problem, as they are the worst. Luckily, a bloke wearing a trilby, who looked high up in their hierarchy, came up to the bar.

'A pint of Guinness.'

'Sorry, I'm not serving you.'

'Why not?'

'Because it's a private party and you shouldn't be here,' I explained.

'But the manager said it was OK. He served us,' he protested.

'He's not the manager; I am,' I corrected him. 'And I'm not serving you.'

I held my breath as he stared at me. I was worried about something happening with my family there in the next bar, but, fortunately, he turned round and followed by the others, walked straight through the bar and out into the street.

Anybody who has had a pub will understand that it is a big problem when a group of Irish Travellers turn up. There is always a menacing atmosphere in the air and, although they are big spenders, they also drive all your regulars out.

One particular Saturday afternoon, loads of them came walking in, all big, menacing-looking blokes.

No way am I serving them, I thought to myself.

'Five pints of Guinness,' the first one to the bar said.

I lifted up the bar flap and walked up to an older bloke with them, who appeared to be the leader. I looked him straight in the eyes and said, 'I'm sorry; I can't serve you.'

'Why not?' he asked. I could feel all their eyes full of hatred on me, but there was no way I could back down.

'We don't serve large groups any more,' I explained.

'Look, we're just gonna have a few drinks and then we'll be on our way,' he assured me.

I knew this was nonsense, so I told him, 'Sorry, I've told you already that we don't serve large groups and I'm not serving you, any of you, now or later.'

It was make or break time.

'OK, thank you very much,' he replied, holding out his hand. I shook his hand, and he turned and walked out of the pub. The others stared at me as if they wanted to lynch me, but, after a few seconds (it seemed like hours), they turned and walked out as well. To be fair to most of the Irish Travellers, if you do not show any fear and are straight with them, they will normally accept it. The people they detest are the ones who hide behind the bar, calling the police.

A local Irish Traveller, known as 'Gypsy John', used to come in the pub every day with his wife and daughter. He was eighty-two years old and always wore a trilby. When it was just these three, it was OK, but different members of their family started paying them visits, and all Irish travellers have got huge families. Whenever a crowd of them came in, General would always make the same remark to Carmel, our Irish barmaid, 'Carmel, can you give us a bit of warning next time your family's coming in?'

She had a great sense of humour and would always laugh.

One Thursday, I was just going out when I looked through

the back windows and saw a group of Travellers in there, clearly having a go at General. I had the chain from the back gate in my hand, I ran up the back stairs, let myself in and then ran downstairs into the pub. The blokes were shouting and swearing and appeared almost hyper.

'I'll tuckin' get on the phone and bring hundreds down here to smash this tuckin' pub up!' one of them screamed.

'What do you mean, you ain't tuckin' serving us?'

Malcolm, Scottish John and Underground Tony were at the other end of the bar, drinking. Malcolm and John would always back us up, even if the odds were stacked against us. General just stood there, looking back at them, which, I felt, was the best tactic. They were itching for trouble and one of them was on his mobile, shouting about 'the tuckin' Duke of Cambridge'.

'And what you tuckin' lookin' at?' the angriest one yelled at me.

I just stood there next to General, looking back at them all the time. They continued making threats as they walked to the door and out of the pub. We never saw them again.

'Gypsy John' would often sit at a different table from his wife and daughter. We noticed that, when Travellers came into the pub, the men and women usually sat at different tables without mixing at all.

Anyway, John's family would come in every day at 11 a.m. and have a few drinks before John went over to the supermarket to buy his cans of Guinness to have with his dinner. They would go home at 1 p.m. to have dinner, and whether it consisted just of Guinness or of something else as well I do not know. They would then return at about 3 p.m.

One morning, John went over the supermarket and returned as normal with his cans of Guinness. However, after a short while, General heard the sound of a can being opened. He walked over to where John was sitting.

'What are you doing, John?' General asked him as John filled his glass up from the can.

'Oh, it's only one can,' John replied.

'Well, it doesn't matter. You can finish that drink and then leave, as we're not serving you any more, General told him.

'After all the money I've spent in here?' protested John.

That was finally the end of our problems with Travellers. We put up a notice on the door saying that we would not serve groups of four or more. On a few occasions, we had some young ones test us, but General, Malcolm or I would go straight over there and tell them. After that, only three at the most would come in to play pool. If they were joined by others, we would go over and tell them immediately. They would only drink Coke and were never a problem.

The one thing about Travellers is that they often get away with a lot through intimidation by numbers or by the threat of numbers. There is no doubt that they are a hard group, but, from what I have seen, they will often back down when confronted, as was the case with Scottish John.

On another occasion, there were three of them by the pool table. Harry was playing against one of them when one of his mates, who was particularly mouthy, started making remarks. Harry was just about to take a shot on the black.

'Ooh, what a lovely arse you've got,' he commented.

Unfortunately for him, Harry missed his shot, so he was in big trouble. Harry threw his cue across the table and turned around.

'What did you say, you bastard?' Harry demanded to know, walking right up to him.

The bloke lost his nerve straight away and ran around the pool table.

'I've a good mind to smash you right in the face,' Harry continued.

The three of them were panicking and ran out of the pub. Twenty seconds later, Harry walked out. I followed him out, just in case, but the three of them were disappearing out of sight.

'What do you want?'
Customer service the Harry way

From left to right; Dapo (from the Insects), Kirpal (tragically died in July 2005), me and Billy (now lives in Australia with his wife and children)

The Duke of Cambridge, Hounslow

Syon School Reunion 2004
Left to right; Brendan Malone, me, Kirpal Rahel, Billy Drinkwater, Lee Garland, Andy Antonio, George Ttoulli, Dapo Ajayi, Andy Newsome and Phil Harding

'We're still standing' - well only just
Left to right; Paul Hill, Nick Shaw, me, Alan Procter and Phil Harding

McCreesh in trouble
Tracey Wood gives General a lift up so he can sort McCreesh out

The Italian Supremes
Left to right; Monica, Sandra and Francesca

Happy 80th Dad!
My mum and I presenting my dad with a cake for each 40 years of his life

'Who wants some?'. Kirpal's asking
Left to right; Malcolm, Gurmit, Kirpal and James

'We've made it!'
Left to right; General, me, young Dave, Rolando, Neilson and Michelle.
Celebrating England's qualification for Euro 2004.

The two Ivors tooled up!
Left to right; Simon, Banana, Deaf Ivor, Ivor the Engine and me.

'I've got my eye on you.'
Me getting to grips with Banana as Kirpal looks on

'Leave my wife alone, Banana!'
Billy attempting to protect his wife Lesley (far right) from Banana's advances
Pawel (far left) and Bucket don't appear to have noticed

Kirpal's Remembrance Do
My mum, General, me and my dad
enjoying our last evening at the pub

Syon Boys
Left to right. Back row: Paul Hill, Billy, Chris Saville, Big Mal and me; front row; Jacko and Nick Shaw

'Are you sure it's only been six years?'
Me reflecting as I play the music for the last time

Nick Ruff gives a seat to an old man
Oz and the boys (and girls) in spring 2002 celebrating a successful season

'You do the three on the left and I'll do the three on the right'
Malcolm giving Big Mark his instructions on the boat to Calais

'OK, John, but please don't nibble my ear'
Scottish John and his wife, Helena

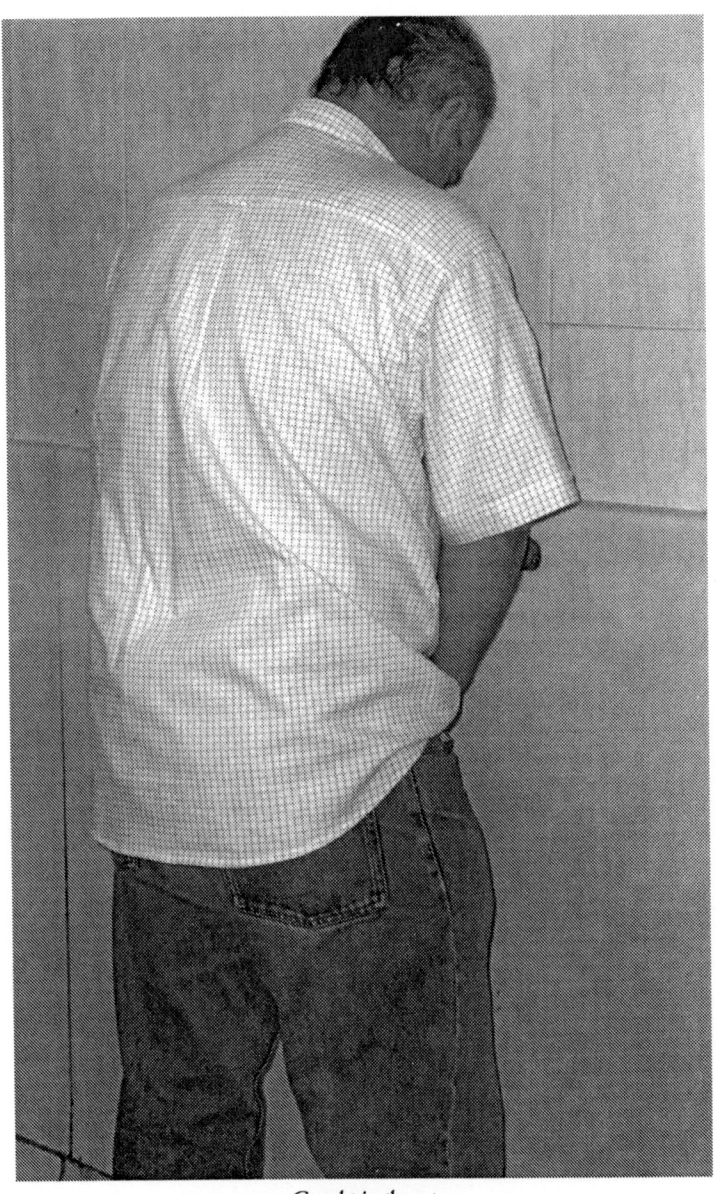

Caught in the act
Nielsen having a crafty fiddle

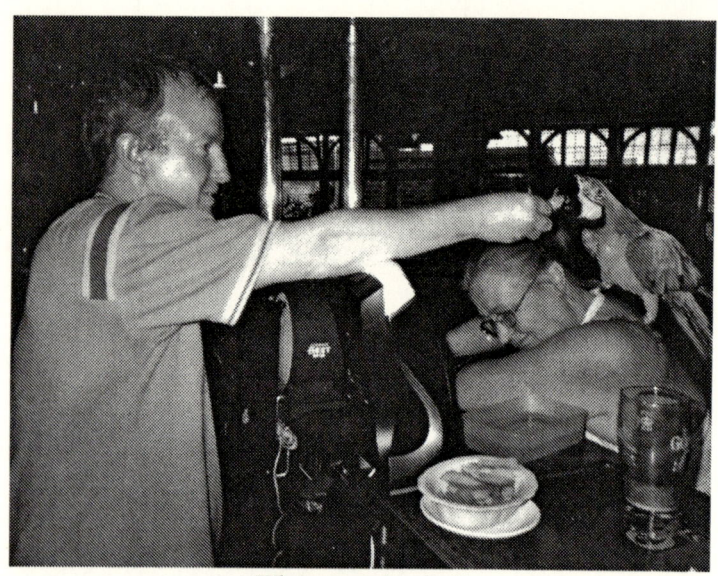

'Who's a pretty boy then?'
Me serving one of our brighter customers in more ways than one!

'You've nothing to brag about boys!'
Left to right; Ralph, Banana and Sean Beddams Adams

Bedfont School Reunion
Left to right: Dave Burvill, Tony Lock, Karl Townsend, Bob Floyd, Joy Best, me, Stephanie Potter, Terry Tomkins and Paul Root

Norma and Livi join the party

'That's very generous of you, Carmel'
Carmel allowing me to rest my chin on a comfortable spot

Left to right: my mum and dad, Ged and General

Another good group of regulars
Back row; James, Liam, Richard and Omar.
Front row; Elise, Jamie and Charlotte

The Three Muskateers: Neilson, General and Scottish James

'Go easy on me Norma.'
Norma with a nervous Richard

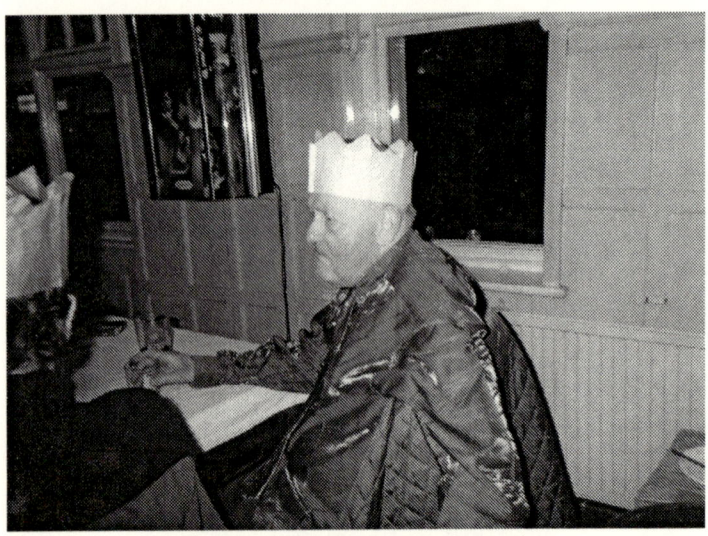

*'Richard, I understand you are depressed
but you have made me even more depressed.'*
A solemn looking Father Peter with Ricardo

Left to right: Finnigan (Keith Goodenough), Peter Horner, Ewelina and Neilson

Left to right: Sue Ellen, JR and Lesley

Father and son
Gurmit and Livi

Grant or Phil? No, it's General

'There's only one hard man in this photo and it's not you Swanny!'
Tony Lock and Swanny

Another quiz night victory for Sister Act
Auntie Joan and Mum

'False alarm; it's not Klaus Barbie, it's Mick Denyer!'

Steady, General

Swanny and General in the early days when we couldn't pay our heating bills

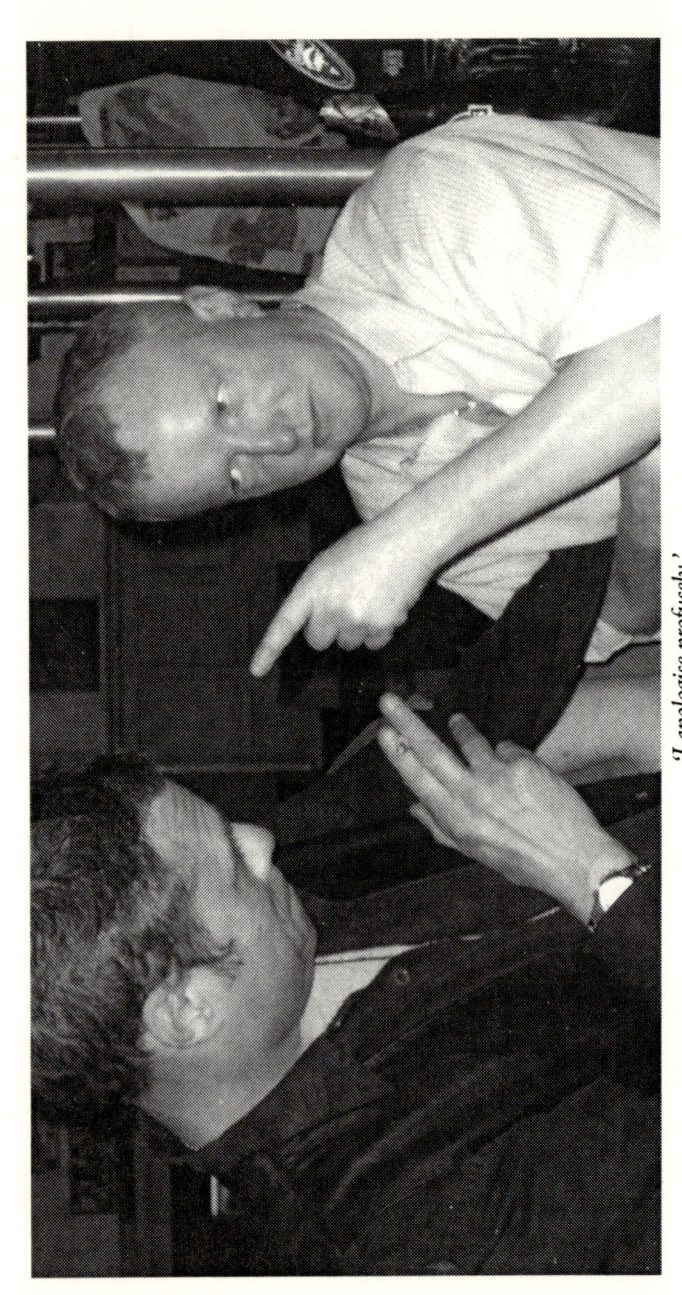

'I apologise profusely.'
I'm giving Ralph one of his many warnings

Gypsy John

Getting back to 'Gypsy John', there were some funny stories involving him. He loved playing pool, and on one occasion he was in the pub with his wife and daughter, who did not play. There was only one other person in the pub: an Irishman of about forty-five.

'Old man, do you want a game of pool?' John suddenly shouted.

I thought I must have misheard him, as there was nobody else in the pub.

'Hey, old man, do you want a game of pool?' John yelled even louder. He was looking directly at the Irishman, who looked behind himself and all around the pub before realising that John was shouting at him. He had a look of utter amazement at the fact that a man in his eighties could be addressing him as 'old man'.

'I say, old man, do you want a game of pool?' John continued, not giving up easily.

The man did not answer him, probably because he had taken offence and felt that the old man did not deserve a reply!

John could not read or write, but short-change him by five pence and he would let you know about it. However, Father Peter once fired a question at John which totally baffled him.

'John, how many children have you got?'

John stared at Father Peter as if he had been asked the most difficult multiplication question. He then turned to his wife for help.

'How many children have we got?'

'Good God, man, don't you even know how many children you've got?' Father Peter scolded him, absolutely horrified.

Father Peter was a master with his use of the English language. For example, he would not refer to Travellers by that name, but would always describe them as 'itinerant people'.

One Saturday, we were watching the football when John came

in with his wife and daughter. I could tell that something was up by the way he approached the bar.

'I need to have a few drinks on the house.'

I'm not sure whether he was asking me or telling me.

'Sorry, John, we do not give out drinks on the house.'

'Go on, just a few.'

'No, John, we can't let you have any drinks. You've got to pay for them like everyone else.'

He looked at me with complete contempt and then turned to Father Peter.

'Father, all I've done is ask Chris for a couple of drinks and he won't give them to me,' he explained, no doubt expecting Father Peter to intervene on his behalf.

'Well, of course he can refuse, John. Chris has got bills to pay. He is not a charity. You should not be asking him, anyway, John, as he is running a business,' scolded Father Peter. 'You have to pay your own way in this life, John.'

John stared at his feet like a schoolboy in the headmaster's office as Father Peter verbally laid into him. I was just beginning to think that somebody had finally got through to him when he looked up and asked Father Peter, 'I don't suppose you could lend me ten pounds, then?'

Father Peter almost choked on his Courage Best.

'Ten pounds? Ten pounds?' he repeated in complete shock. 'John, I haven't got ten pounds.'

'How about five pounds, then?' John persisted, failing to get the message.

'John, I haven't got any money to give you. I will stand you a drink. Chris, get John a pint of Guinness.'

I walked along the bar, glad that Father Peter had put John in his place, but a bit taken aback that he was buying him a drink. I reached up for the glass, but was interrupted by Father Peter shouting, 'Chris, make it a half!'

Gypsy John looked like a small boy who had had his tube of Smarties taken away from him!

Father Peter was, as you would expect from a Jesuit, an extremely intelligent man who had taught Latin, Ancient Greek, Russian and English. He, like Kirpal, never talked down to anybody and would always patiently answer any questions, however ridiculous they were.

He would insist on having no froth whatsoever on his Courage Best and would continuously whack people with his stick. After having been hit for the fourth time, Tony Baloney had had enough.

'If he wasn't an old priest, I'd knock his block off!' he insisted.

Father Peter would sometimes go round to the café side of the pub to have a bite to eat with his pint and would often have a little afternoon nap. On one occasion, he had had a meal and a few pints and had begun dozing off when Banana went to put something in the fridge out the back. She was only gone about five seconds before hearing the door go, so she rushed back in, expecting to have another customer. However, she realised that Father Peter was not there, and when she went to look out of the window, she saw him boarding his bus on the other side of the road. He had never moved so quickly! He was the only person to ever 'do a runner' from the café without paying his bill; a pure accident, of course!

If you are reading this, Father Peter, do not worry, as it came out of Banana's wages!

Old Bill

On one of the many occasions we were having a 'late one', West Ham Roland came back in from the porch, where he had been on his mobile.

'There's Old Bill outside!' he warned. 'Right, be quiet, everyone!'

'Shh, Old Bill outside!' was whispered from person to person.

I sneaked a look from behind the blind out of the side window and saw three of them at the front door.

'Quickly, everyone, down the cellar!' I instructed. General directed them like a traffic policeman and they all went rushing down there, clutching their drinks. I also noticed that Banana had gone running down there with them, which I thought was a bit unnecessary, as she lived and worked at the pub, so she did not have to justify why she was there.

We cleared some glasses and I went to the door, as they were hammering on it.

'Good evening. We were just wondering whether everything is OK.'

'Yeah, everything's fine. Any particular reason?' I asked.

'No, not really. We're just doing some checks in the area.'

'No, it's been fine. I'm just off to bed.'

'OK, well, don't let us stop you. Good night.'

'What a strange conversation,' I mumbled to myself as I closed the door. I realised that it was probably a warning that they knew what was going on and that we should not push things too far.

'It's OK, they've gone,' General announced to the drinkers down in the cellar. They had never been so quiet. They seemed to be happy enough down there.

'Who is this "Old Bill"?' Tiziana asked me later.

'You mean "who are the Old Bill?" ' I corrected her, as I was always trying to help her with her English.

'No, I mean this man, Bill, who came to the pub earlier. He

must be really big and strong, as everyone seemed scared of him. Even Malcolm, Big Mark and Roland went down the cellar to hide from him!'

'Yeah, you are right. This "Old Bill" is a giant, really strong and mad! Everyone's scared of him!' I enthused, watching with amusement the look of horrified fascination on Banana's face.

'What did you say to him then?'

'I told him nobody was here and gave him a hundred pounds so he would go,' I joked.

'A hundred pounds! *Mamma mia!*' she screamed in astonishment.

It did not take long for Banana to find out that 'Old Bill' was not a giant, raving lunatic terrorising everyone, but a term used to describe the police.

The police probably turned up fewer than ten times in the six years I was involved with the pub. Generally, they were very supportive, and I now have more sympathy for them, through having had to deal with some of the same scum as them. In my teens and early twenties, I was beaten up by them on a few occasions and stitched up in court as well, so I had every reason to mistrust them. However, coming into contact with some of the vermin they have to deal with made me appreciate them a bit more. On the other hand, there were a couple of occasions on which they behaved like incompetent idiots.

One incident that springs to mind was one Friday night. We were holding a pool competition and had eighteen names in the hat. We did the draw, with the result being that four players had to play in a qualifying match to get it to the correct number: sixteen for a knockout. Therefore, we pulled the four names required from the hat, or, to be more precise, from a pint glass.

'That ain't fair,' commented one of the four.

'What's not fair?' I asked.

'That I've got to play an extra game.'

'Well, so have three others, and they're not complaining about it,' responded Malcolm, who had done the draw with me.

'It's a fix,' he continued.

'Oh, yeah, we fixed it so that General had to play an extra game as well,' I retorted.

'Yeah, OK, but then why us four?' asked brains of Britain.

'Fuckin' hell, mate, it's only a pound,' I exclaimed, becoming exasperated. 'If you don't wanna play, we'll give you your pound back.'

'Just fuckin' play the game!' chimed in Scottish John.

The sight of Malcolm and John getting annoyed with him was enough to shut the idiot up for ten minutes.

We had a set of pub cues for public use, although some of the regulars had their own cues, which they kept behind the bar for their personal use or for their mates. General used Malcolm's own cue and thrashed Mr Big Mouth.

'That weren't fair; he used his own cue,' he ranted.

'Look, give it a rest, will you, mate? If you want to bring in your own cue next time, nobody's stopping you,' I explained.

'It's a fuckin' con,' he commented continuously to anyone within ear range.

'OK, time to go,' I told him, trying not to lose my temper.

'Why?'

'Because you're pissing everyone off and you've been a right pain in the arse all night.' Diplomacy has not always been my best attribute.

'I don't see why—'

'Come on, out you go,' Malcolm said, guiding him to the door. Within a second, he had gone and the door was closed behind him. We got on with the competition and had a relaxing night.

After everyone had gone home, Gurmit and I were still in the mood for a drink, so we sat up, drinking and chatting until 3.30 p.m. I let Gurmit out and started to clear our glasses away. I nearly jumped out of my skin when the phone started ringing.

'Hello,' I mumbled, half asleep.

'It's the police outside. Open the door.'

'Yeah, all right; who is it?'

'It is the police. If you come and look out of the window, you will see a blue flashing light. Now open the door.'

I went to the door and had barely unlocked it when the door flew open and in they charged like the cavalry, knocking me flying.

'Oh, come in!' I shouted sarcastically. 'You can calm down; there's only me here!'

The inspector was barking out the orders while totally ignoring me.

'You check the toilets, you look behind the bar, you this, you that, you the other…'

'Excuse me, do you mind telling me what's going on?' I enquired.

He spun round and looked at me. I had the feeling that he had forgotten all about me as he had been having such fun.

'We have had an allegation made that a member of the public was threatened earlier this evening, in this pub, by a man with a firearm.'

'When is this supposed to have happened?' I asked, convinced that I must have been dreaming.

'An allegation has been made that a pool competition was rigged and, when the person who made the complaint to us pointed it out, he was threatened with a gun by a man called Eric.'

That meant that not only had Malcolm changed his name to Eric, but he had been playing pool with a shotgun as well.

'Now, I know what this is all about…' I started to say.

'Before you go any further, just consider yourself very lucky that the Armed Response Unit was not called here.'

'The Armed Response Unit?'

'Yes; it was only at the last moment that we made the decision to come in here unarmed.'

'Nobody was armed in here tonight, or on any other night, for that matter. Well, only with pool cues, and that wasn't to hit anyone with.'

I went on to explain the night's events to him, but he did not appear to be the slightest bit interested. I was interrupted by the various officers returning to report their findings.

'Nothing,' they said, one after another.

'What about upstairs?' the inspector asked.

'You must be joking; my nephews and niece are asleep up there.'

'OK, but consider yourself lucky and take this as a warning.'

What was that supposed to mean? How ridiculous is a system

in which somebody can phone from a public phone under a fictitious name, make an allegation against a person, or a place, and have the police react in this way and then tell me that I am lucky and that this was a warning?

Another point is that if that idiot, or anyone else, for that matter, had been threatened by a gun, then surely the police should not have taken nearly six hours to come and check it out. Also, what would have happened if I had been up in bed and not answered the door? I think I know the answer to that one.

Another occasion when the police were on a go-slow was one Wednesday Quiz Night. A group of French students were in the bar. They, like all the other groups of French who visited the pub, were polite and friendly. After about an hour, one of the girls approached me and told me that her jacket had been stolen. She showed me where she had put it, which was on the sofa next to where they were all sitting. However, I had already noticed a shifty-looking couple sitting nearby and knew instinctively that they had taken it. The bloke was a Londoner and seemed really dodgy, and the girl was Irish and very rough and ready. Besides this, they kept fiddling about with a bag, which they had under the table.

'Excuse me; one of the group over there left a jacket on this sofa. You haven't seen it, by any chance, have you?'

Their reaction was the worst bit of acting I had seen in years.

'No; no, I haven't seen a jacket; have you?' the woman asked the bloke.

'Jacket? No, I haven't seen one either,' he said.

'Look, are you sure?' I asked impatiently.

'Of course we're tuckin' sure,' the woman replied, on the defensive.

'What about in your bag, then?'

'Are you accusing us of nicking it?' she shouted aggressively.

I was bursting to say, *Yes, you fuckin' bitch, I am*, but instead I replied, 'I haven't accused you of anything. I'm just asking.'

'That's just tuckin' grand, that is. We're just sitting here having a couple of beers, and you come over and accuse us of nicking a jacket. Look, I've got a tuckin' jacket here: my tuckin' jacket!' she ranted.

'Yeah, mate, what's your problem?' the man chimed in. I had wondered when he was going to join in.

'I'll tell you what my problem is, mate: I want that jacket back.'

'It ain't yours, is it?'

'Excuse me, I have to say that neither of these have moved from this table since they came in,' intervened an Irishman called Jimmy, who was sitting on the next table. He was a decent bloke, a schoolteacher who came in every week for the quiz. However, I hope that he is a bit more alert to the wrongdoings of his pupils.

Amazingly, the woman got the wrong end of the stick, thinking that Jimmy was accusing them rather than defending them.

'You cheeky bastard! What yer tryin' to say? You mind yer own business.'

Jimmy's face was a picture. *Serves you right*, I was thinking whilst trying not to laugh.

'OK, let's forget all about it,' I said, although what I really wanted to do was grab their bag, give the French girl her jacket back and throw these thieves out of the pub. However, as you know, in this day and age it would have been me and not them appearing in court. Therefore, at about 8 p.m. I had to do something that I hated doing, and that was telling the barman to call the police.

After explaining to the French students precisely what was happening, I continued with the quiz. I pretended not to be paying any attention to the couple under suspicion, but made up my mind that, if they got up to leave, I would lock the door and refuse to let them out until the matter was resolved.

I kept my eye on them discreetly, though, and was relieved to see them get a couple more drinks. This meant that they would be staying a while. They had relaxed again and obviously thought that they had got away with it. Anyway, the clock was ticking away and they were getting more intoxicated. However, as the police still had not turned up, we knew we had to continue serving them so that they did not become suspicious. The barman phoned them again and was told that they were on their way.

At 10.45 p.m., the police finally arrived. There were two ordinary coppers, a PC and a WPC, who were fine. However, once again, there was a boss accompanying them who was completely out of touch with reality.

I explained to the WPC what had occurred that evening, so she and her colleague approached the couple.

'Do you mind if we take a look in your bag, as we are looking for a jacket that is missing?'

'Why? We don't want you looking in our bag.'

'Look, if you've got nothing to hide, then you may as well show us.'

A struggle ensued, and the couple reacted aggressively and were promptly arrested. The jacket was found in the bag, as expected, which delighted the French girl. I was also relieved, as we very rarely had anything like that occurring in the pub.

The couple ended up getting arrested for 'Drunk and Disorderly'. They could not get charged with theft, as nobody had actually seen which one of them had put the jacket in the bag!

The sergeant ushered me aside.

'We are arresting them for "Drunk and Disorderly".'

'OK.'

'Haven't you got anything else to say for yourself?' he asked.

'I beg your pardon?'

'Letting that pair get so drunk on your premises. I consider that very irresponsible behaviour,' he lectured.

'Hold on a minute,' I replied, in total disbelief. 'The only reason they are so drunk is because it took you nearly three hours to get here. The only way we could keep them here was to continue serving them.' I could, of course, have detained them, but that would, no doubt, have resulted in my getting charged.

'You know that it is an offence to serve somebody who is drunk or who appears to be drunk?' he continued, obviously oblivious to what I had just explained to him. I repeated myself, but it went straight over his head. I suspect that, in these days of political correctness, in which the police force has totally lost its way, he will go far. Any situations that arose after the above two incidents were dealt with by ourselves. Do you blame us?

A Few Wind-Ups

One particular Monday night, General was on top form. He had been mixing Guinness with Port all night. Port was Kirpal's favourite tipple, and he had persuaded General to go on it. A reluctant General had eventually given in when Kirpal placed a large one in front of him.

Rab was working behind the bar and our group consisted of Neilson, Banana, Kirpal, Gurmit, General and me.

'Sue Ellen, you're a drunk and unfit mother!' Gurmit shouted at Banana. 'Sue Ellen' was his nickname for Banana, who, in turn, always referred to him as 'JR'.

'Shut up and beehive!' Banana never realised that the correct word was 'behave'.

'And comb your hair, Sue Ellen; it's always a mess, or you'll never work in this town again!' Gurmit, aka JR, scolded.

General was listing his demands for appearing in the starring role in a film about British rule in India, for which Kirpal was doing the research. However, he was taken aback when Kirpal informed him that the only 'lines' he would have in the film would be to shout 'Fire!'

He eventually fell asleep at the bar. Tiziana tried waking him, which was more of a task than she expected. She finally had some success and helped him off his stool, but had to grab him as his legs gave way beneath him.

'Come on, General, stand up!' she ordered him. 'Good boy! Right, you walk and I'll follow you to make sure that you don't fall over.'

General obeyed Tiziana's instructions and made his way through the bar in a daze, almost as if he were sleepwalking, while Banana walked behind him with her arms outstretched, preventing him from falling backwards. They headed towards the bottom of the stairs in the dark. I caught up with them and motioned for Banana to let me take her place. We changed places swiftly, though General was oblivious to what was happening anyway. He staggered up the stairs, while I supported his back to stop him tumbling back down. 'Thanks, Banana!' General was mumbling continuously as we mounted each step. 'Thanks, Banana,' he murmured yet again as we entered the bathroom in the dark. I then started groping his chest and running my hands all over his body.

'Oh, Banana!' he commented enthusiastically, sounding more awake than he had done for hours. He turned around and I continued groping him as his eyes struggled to focus in the dark. Suddenly, he realised it was not Banana touching him, but me!

'You fucker!' he yelled, in the clearest English he had spoken all night. He continued with the insults as I went back downstairs, laughing my head off!

General used his talent for putting on accents to good use in a classic wind-up on Ralph. It was a Friday night, and Duncan, who was a really placid bloke until he was on about his sixth pint, began picking an argument with Ralph. Ralph was a really complex, likeable bloke, whose usual way of starting a sentence would be, 'I've got three ex-wives and...', sounding like Ross in *Friends*! He was always dressed in a shirt, waistcoat, jeans and boots and on more than one occasion came in wearing a Stetson. He would have been more at home in Houston than Hounslow!

'Where have you parked your horse, Ralph?' Gurmit would yell out at the top of his voice.

Ralph spent most of his time in the pub saying 'I apologise profusely' if he thought that he had offended or upset anyone in any way. However, on this occasion, he was having none of it and began shouting at Duncan.

'Look, leave me alone. I've just come in for a quiet drink.'
'But, Ralph, I'm just trying to tell you—' mumbled Duncan.
'Go away!' yelled Ralph.
'Now, you listen to me,' Duncan responded.
'Look, Duncan, I apologise if I've upset you, but I just wanna be on my own.'
'You bastard!' Duncan growled, lunging at Ralph.
'Right, come on, Duncan; time to go,' I announced, while guiding Duncan to the door.

'Why do I have to go?'

'Because you've had too much to drink and it's time to go.' I had been through this scenario a thousand times with Duncan.

I locked the door behind him and went back inside to hear Ralph telling everyone in the pub, 'I don't know why, but whatever I do or say seems to offend Duncan.'

'You're always picking on him, Ralph!' Gurmit remarked, winding him up.

'No, definitely not!' shouted Ralph. 'I always bend over backwards to be civil to him, but it only seems to make him angrier.'

General had sneaked upstairs while this conversation was going on. The phone rang, and Rab answered it.

'Ralph, it's Duncan for you.'

'What's he want now?' Ralph complained, taking the phone.

'Hello, Duncan, how can I help you?'

'Well look, I apologise if I offended you...' Ralph said, trying to pacify an obviously irate Duncan.

'Duncan, I'm trying to apologise here!' he exclaimed, losing patience with the difficult Duncan. 'Well, I'll tell you what, perhaps it's better if we don't talk to each other any more, as all I seem to do is antagonise you.'

General was upstairs, playing a blinder imitating Duncan on the phone, and Ralph had fallen for it hook, line and sinker. General told us afterwards that he would be all nice to Ralph, then, whenever Ralph said anything he would shout down the phone, 'Nooh, Ralph, nooh!'

'OK, I'm on my way!' Ralph yelled angrily before slamming down the receiver. He walked over to his stool and started putting his jacket on.

'Where are you going, Ralph?' asked General, who had reappeared in the pub.

'I'm going over the kebab shop to fight Duncan!' explained Ralph.

'You're doing what?' I asked, noticing General disappear again.

'I've just told you. I'm going over the kebab shop to sort it out with Duncan once and for all. I've tried being nice to him, but, if he wants to sort it out this way, then I've got no choice. Right, let me out!' Ralph insisted.

The phone rang again as Ralph marched towards the exit.

'Ralph, it's Duncan for you!' shouted Banana.

'I'm on my way over now, Duncan,' yelled Ralph down the phone. 'You're where? Well, bollocks to that, then!' he shouted as he slammed down the receiver yet again.

He took off his jacket, sat down and started supping his pint.

'Aren't you going over the kebab shop to fight Duncan, then, Ralph?' Billy asked joining in the fun.

'No, I'm not, because he just phoned back to say that he's waiting at a kebab shop in Isleworth and not that one over the road, and I'm not going all the way to Isleworth at this time of night to fight Duncan,' he shouted, almost at boiling point.

'Ralph, calm down!' General ordered, reappearing in the bar again.

'I apologise profusely, General, but Duncan's really wound me up!' explained an irate Ralph.

Everyone who was still in the pub was sitting at the bar, and they were all by now aware that it had been General and not Duncan on the other end of the line. Everyone was trying to keep a straight face.

'Lend us your mobile,' General said to me, and this time he only went into the other bar to make the call.

'Duncan, stop bothering Ralph. He doesn't want to speak to you,' scolded Banana.

'No, give it here; I'll speak to him!' Ralph screamed, rushing to the phone 'OK, Duncan. Yes, I am listening. Well, I'm sorry you've been waiting there, but I'm not coming all the way to Isleworth to fight you.'

General walked into the bar where we all were and continued to mimic Duncan down the phone right in front of Ralph, who, incredibly, failed to notice and continued arguing with 'Duncan'.

We could not hold it any longer and we all burst out laughing. With a puzzled look on his face, Ralph looked along the bar at everyone laughing before he suddenly noticed General standing in front of him, talking in a Scottish accent. Ralph's face was a picture as it suddenly dawned on him that it was General on the other end of the phone and not Duncan.

'OK, I fell for that one. Get everyone a drink from me!' Ralph shouted, being a great sport. He then shocked us with his next question, 'How many of the calls were from Duncan and how many were from General?', which showed how much General had confused him.

Duncan was one of the many Scots who were regulars in the Duke. He was generally very pleasant, but a pain when drunk. At one private party, Duncan was enjoying the chilli so much that he did not go to the trouble of using a knife and fork, but instead picked up the bowl and attempted to tip the chilli directly down his throat. Unfortunately, most of it ended up all over his face, so he looked like he was wearing a mud pack!

He had a very nice girlfriend called Collette, although it was a very volatile relationship, as one week she would be taking him to court and the next week they would be all over each other again! On the frequent occasions on which Duncan had upset Collette, Richard or Ged would take him into the corner for a pep talk. Ricardo in particular would give him a severe ticking-off.

'Big Danny' and 'little Danny' were father and son and two Scots you would not want to argue with; 'little Danny' was, in fact, about twenty stone. They were great blokes and fitted in really well with Malcolm, Big Mark, Harry, Steve and the other regulars.

On one occasion, Big Mark and Mal were giving Scottish Dave some stick during an England match, just as four big Scottish blokes walked into the pub and began ordering drinks behind where Dave was sitting.

'Can you hear the Scotland sing? I can't hear a fuckin' thing!' Mal and Big Mark sang, oblivious to the Scottish blokes glaring directly at them. General stepped in to defuse it and Dave backed him up.

'Oh, no, we're all mates in here. We're all just having a laugh. I want them to win, really!'

'That's fine then,' the four Scots replied, immediately relaxing.

Another Scot was Rab, who eventually worked behind the bar for a while. Like the whole country, we were delighted when England avenged previous famous defeats at the hands of Argentina by beating them 1–0 in Japan in 2002. The only disappointing thing about it was that it was not an evening kick-off. That would have been even more fantastic. Rab watched the game in the pub with us and, like the other Scots in the pub, Scottish John, Richard, Dave, James, Duncan and 'Terry the Busker', had been cheering England on. Andy Murray, take note! Malcolm, one of the most patriotic Englishman you could ever meet, announced that he was going on a pub crawl around Hounslow to celebrate our victory. I declined an invitation to join him, as I knew it was going to be a long day and that I would have to keep an eye on everything.

'I'll come with you, Malcolm,' Rab shouted excitedly.

'Don't forget, you're working at seven, Rab,' I reminded him.

'Don't worry, Chris, I'll be drinking Coke anyway,' he assured me.

At 6.55 p.m. Malcolm came into the pub with a grin from ear to ear, followed by Rab, who succeeded in knocking into every chair and table between the entrance and the bar.

'He's completely out of his box,' announced Malcolm.

'Oh, yeah,' I replied, smiling. 'I'm not falling for that one.'

'Honestly, Chris, he's well bladdered,' Malcolm insisted.

After a few moments I realised that it was not a wind-up and that he was really drunk. I had already been drinking, but, fortunately, General had not and got behind the bar. Rab's wife, Eleanor, rang up a few times, but we tried to cover for him by saying that he was down in the cellar, that he was over at the shop, that he had gone to the toilet and so on.

'Look, I know he's there and I know he's been drinking,' she snapped, obviously fed up with our excuses.

Despite our denials, she did not believe us and, ten minutes later, a cab pulled up outside with Eleanor in the back. She entered the pub with a face like thunder and headed straight for Rab. She gave him a right ticking-off, although he just stood there, grinning. Eleanor then grabbed him and started shoving him towards the door.

'Rab is going home, he's going home, he's going home, he's going; Rab is going home, he's going home…' we all sang at the top of our voices, to the tune of 'Three Lions'. Rab returned after about five minutes and, much to our surprise, Eleanor had stormed off home.

About half an hour later, Ralph staggered to the bar and motioned General over.

'If Eleanor calls, tell her I haven't been in here all evening,' he mumbled nervously.

We could not believe that he was so drunk that he could not even remember Eleanor being in the pub only half an hour earlier. Rab got loads of stick about that night for ages. He seemed slightly embarrassed by the fact that he had celebrated England's victory with more enthusiasm than any Englishman we knew!

Eleanor was fuming about that night for ages and blamed me for a lot of it, as I had been covering up for Rab. I should have kept my guard up, as I was now on her hit list.

A few months later, I went downstairs one morning to collect the post, and amongst the usual dreaded bills was a handwritten envelope. I opened it to find a letter that said something like the following:

Dear Chris,

I am writing this letter to let you know how attracted I am to you, blah, blah, blah...

I will not be happy until we are together as one. Please do not deprive me of my one chance of happiness.

All my love,

Martin

I had started reading the letter quite happily, being curious to know which girl was writing this to me. However, as I got to the end of the letter and realised that my secret admirer was a man, I was not quite so happy, to say the least. I took it upstairs to show General.

'Is it Irish Martin, the one...?'

'It must be,' I replied. 'He's the only Martin I can think of who drinks in here. He seems a bit dodgy as well,' I added.

'Don't worry about it; I'll sort him out,' General told me.

Later that day, I went downstairs and there, propping up the bar, as smug as ever, was Martin. I gave him a filthy look and went back upstairs.

'The smug bastard's down in the bar, acting as if he hasn't got a care in the world,' I complained to General.

'I'll go and speak to him now, then,' General assured me.

He went down immediately and beckoned Martin into the corridor. He must have wondered what General wanted him for, as they had never previously passed the time of day to each other.

'Martin, why did you send Chris a letter?' General asked, getting straight to the point.

'Send Chris a letter? What sort of letter?' Martin stuttered nervously.

'Look, don't give me that rubbish. You know full well what sort of letter,' General retorted. 'Chris is really angry about it, so you'd better make sure you don't send any more or there'll be big trouble.'

'It was definitely him. He went bright red when I spoke to him about it,' General explained to me after coming back upstairs.

Fortunately, Martin stopped coming into the pub so often, so it appeared that the ticking-off General had given him had worked.

A couple of weeks later, a group of us were having a late drink when the discussion turned to wind-ups.

'Eleanor's a great wind-up!' enthused Rab.

'You couldn't get Chris,' claimed Banana.

'Oh, he's easy. I've already got him,' Eleanor announced with great pride.

'Oh, yeah; when?' I asked doubtfully.

'What about your secret admirer, Martin, then?' she asked.

I looked at her in disbelief. It was incredible, as Eleanor had not known anything about Martin's bizarre behaviour but had chosen that name at random because, as she put it, 'None of the regulars are called Martin.'

I held my hands up and admitted that she had well and truly got me on that one! God knows what Martin had thought General was on about!

A Couple of Nuisances

Martin started to come back into the pub after a while, and General and I were a bit friendlier to him, as we felt a bit guilty after our accusation. Incredibly, he never mentioned the incident, which was a bit strange. It was not long, though, before he started upsetting people again.

There were two girls staying above the pub: one called Aisha, who used to work as a barmaid, and her friend Vicky, who had never been out of Glasgow before. They were staying for a long weekend and, on the Saturday night, were having a few drinks with Malcolm and Scottish John. Martin was nearby and kept butting into the conversation.

'You've got a lovely pair of tits!' Martin commented to Aisha for the third time in ten minutes. He had also made similar remarks to Vicky.

'OK, cut it out now!' she snapped back at him.

'There's no need to be embarrassed about them. They are perfect, and the nipples poke through nicely as well!' Martin enthused, obviously not getting the message.

'Shut yer mouth now and apologise to the girls!' Malcolm ordered him, finally losing his patience.

'Bollocks, I'm not fuckin'—' Martin shouted defiantly.

'Right, outside now!' Malcolm shouted, giving Martin a shove. Martin went flying and landed in a heap on the floor. Imagine what would have happened if Malcolm had actually hit him.

Afterwards, Martin was virtually in tears as he ranted to anybody who could be bothered to listen to him.

'He doesn't realise who he's messing with. I know some really influential people in the IRA and I'm going to get them down here to sort that bastard out!'

'I don't think so, Martin.' I said, smiling, as I had heard it all before.

'I fuckin' will!' he insisted.

'Yeah, whatever you say.'

He lived in a fantasy world. He continued coming into the pub, but was petrified of Malcolm and would always sit as far away from him as possible. He would frequently glance over nervously at Malcolm to check where he was. Not long after this, the headless corpse of a girl who had drunk in our pub on a few occasions was found in the River Thames. I think her name was Zoe. Martin started bragging that he had slept with her the weekend before she disappeared. As he was a complete weirdo, some of the regulars began to suspect that he could have had something to do with her murder.

There was another Irish nutcase by the name of Rosie who drank in the pub. She was an Irish woman from a Travelling background who was well known in the Hounslow area. She was very generous and could be good company until she had sunk a few drinks, and then she would become argumentative and aggressive.

One evening, she came into the pub and was acting strangely, which, for her, was really saying something. Pat, a big, black lady who always reminded me of Mammy Two-Shoes in *Tom and Jerry*, came up to the bar. She was a really lovely, happy, bubbly lady who tragically died a couple of years later. She was the one who had threatened to bash Esther up if she caused Banana any more problems. Whenever she walked into the pub, the place would light up immediately. However, on this occasion, she had a worried look on her face.

'What's up, Pat? You're looking a bit serious this evening,' I remarked.

'Chris, don't look now, but see that woman sitting at the window? She's got a gun on her—'

'Got a gun—?'

'Shh, not so loud. She's a right nutter! She told me she's got a gun and she's gonna hold up Eurofoods over the road.'

I had no reason whatsoever to doubt Pat, as she was neither a drama queen nor a liar. Besides, I also knew that Rosie was a bit of a lunatic, and that is an understatement. A few weeks earlier, on my birthday, she had threatened three Italian friends in the ladies' toilets and, when I had a go at her about it, she had replied, 'But don't you understand, Chris? I was protecting you from them.'

'You couldn't make up what goes on in here,' I commented to Pat, as I served her usual drink of brandy and Babycham with two lumps of ice.

'I know what you mean, Chris. I wouldn't want your job for any amount of money,' she remarked sympathetically.

I approached Rosie. 'Hello, Rosie; how are you?' I asked cheerfully.

There was a glazed, vacant look in her eyes.

'I'm tuckin' pissed off!'

'What's up, then?'

'I've found out today that I'm not allowed to see my kids any more.'

'Where are they, then, Rosie?' I enquired. I had never heard her mention her kids before.

'They're in Blackpool.'

'How many children?'

'Four, and, if I can't see them, some bastard's gonna pay for it!' she screamed, attracting everyone in the pub's attention, which added to the tension.

'What are you gonna do, then?' I asked.

'I told you. I'm gonna make some bastard pay for it. Like him over there!' she threatened.

'Who?'

'I've told you already. That bastard in that shop over there.'

'Why; what's he done?' I asked, failing to see the connection between social workers in Blackpool and a shopkeeper in Hounslow.

'He wouldn't let me have any tuckin' beer, the bastard!' she yelled.

'Why not?'

'Because I haven't got any money,' she shouted menacingly.

'Would you like a drink, Rosie?' I asked her, not wanting to join the bloke from Eurofoods on her hit list.

'A Foster's please,' she replied.

'A Foster's and a pint of Guinness, please, Harry. I may as well have a last pint if I'm gonna get shot!' I said, only half jokingly.

'She hasn't got a gun, surely?' asked Harry.

'I dunno, but I ain't gonna take any chances with a nutter like her,' I replied, not taking my eyes off Rosie for a moment. I had also made up my mind to make a dive for her if she tried to put her hand in her inside pocket. Knowing my luck, she would only be getting her lighter!

'It looks like there's a bulge there,' commented Harry, whose brother Steve was also there. They were always very loyal if there was any trouble.

'Here you are, Rosie,' I said, handing her a pint of Foster's.

She was still ranting about 'those bastards in Eurofoods' as I sat down again. I had got to know the two blokes who had been running it, as they used to come over to the pub for a game of pool and a few drinks. They were Sri Lankans, called Deep and Xavier, and were always polite and friendly. They would not stand any nonsense in their shop and, on one occasion, Deep chased a huge black bloke all the way to the tube station, after he ran off without paying for cigarettes, and brought him down with a karate kick in the back.

Over the next couple of hours, we continued chatting. She would appear to have calmed down, only to then explode into anger once again. I had had a glimpse of what looked like a gun and was not going to let her out of my sight. Fortunately, we were sitting near the bar, so I could get the drinks in without straying too far from her. I was also dying to go to the toilet, but that would have to wait a while, as I did not want to leave her. Somebody then whispered to me about calling the police.

'Not yet. We don't really need armed police swarming all over the place.'

Scouse Steve knew what I meant, as we had been trying hard to improve the image of the pub and did not really need that sort of adverse publicity.

I got two more drinks in. I was beginning to feel the effect of the beer and was also bursting to go to the toilet.

'Let me have the gun, Rosie.'

'No tuckin' way!' she insisted, eyes blazing.

We continued talking. I was sure that I could have jumped on her and wrestled the gun from her, but I did not fancy her returning the next day with another gun, firing all over the place in revenge.

Eventually, we used the 'softly, softly' approach. Scouse Steve went around, quietly asking everyone to drink up and leave, while I kept her attention. After everyone had gone, we pointed out to her that it was time to go. Eurofoods was in darkness by then.

'I'll only go if you walk me up the road,' Rosie said.

'Of course I will,' I replied, relieved that she would finally be leaving.

'Walk me to the back of the flats round the back of the Kentucky. There's a party there tonight.'

'Come in and have a drink,' she suggested, when we arrived at the flats.

'No, thanks, Rosie, I can't,' I insisted. I can not remember what excuse I made, but it was a feeble one. I could imagine what sort of party it would have been: half a dozen winos with a few cans of Tennants Extra between them. I rushed off before she had a chance to realise what was going on.

Scouse Steve, Harry and General all had big grins on their faces as I walked back into the pub, but they were disappointed to find out that Rosie had not made me do anything at gunpoint!

Banana's Café

We were always joking that Banana ran her café like a dictator. Actually, it was no joke, because she did! The café was in the old public bar, which my dad and Finnigan converted, and they did a brilliant job.

Banana was like an Italian, female version of Basil Fawlty. She would be really rude to the regulars, who lapped it up. One day, my mate Billy walked in, only to receive a typical Banana welcome.

'I hope you don't want anything to eat!' she shouted at him, the moment he walked through the door. She was very flustered, as she had been really busy.

'I'm sorry, but I was under the impression that this was a café,' replied a bemused Billy.

'Well, make yourself useful and go and get the papers for me,' she demanded.

Billy returned with the papers and sat down to read one.

'Billy, what do you think you are doing?' Banana yelled at him.

'I'm reading the paper,' replied the astonished Billy.

'Not that. I mean, why are you sitting at that table?'

Billy looked around at the other tables and then back at Banana in amazement. 'Why shouldn't I sit here, then?'

'Because you should be sitting by the window, where people can see you!' she commanded.

'I might not want people to see me,' responded Billy.

'Look, just do as you are told, Billy!' ordered the impatient Banana.

On another occasion, she asked Billy to go down the high street to buy something and then produced a long list. Billy returned about an hour later.

'Billy, they are all the wrong size! Go back and change them!' was Banana's response.

She would stand by regulars with her hands on hips, insisting that they eat every bit of salad.

'Come on, eat it up. It's good for you,' she would insist.

She once gave Ralph a severe ticking-off for not finishing his baked beans, so, after that, Ralph used to hide his leftovers under a serviette. He was off the hook for a while, until Banana made a chance discovery when I moved the serviette! Ralph got a right dressing-down for that. He discovered a far safer method of disposing of anything left on his plate, and that was by calling upon the services of Malcolm, the pub's human dustbin, who would eat anything! That went well for a while, until General spilt the beans and Ralph was once again in Banana's bad books.

General and his kids, Christian, Glenn and Shannon, brought Banana a present back from their holiday in Tenerife. It was a bell with 'Tenerife' on it, and Banana started ringing it every night to notify customers of last orders in the café.

'Last orders for the foo-ood!' she would announce at the top of her voice.

On one particular evening, she went over to chat to Gurmit, Kirpal and Malcolm at the end of the bar. Gurmit pinched the cockle out of the bell, then picked it up and started shaking it.

'Banana, this bell's not working!' declared Gurmit.

'Don't be silly, Gurmit, of course it is. Give it here.' Banana demanded, taking the bell and trying to ring it. 'Oh no, what's happened to it?' she asked no one in particular, her hands waving all over the place.

'Here you are, Banana; this was lying on the floor,' said the lying Gurmit, handing the missing cockle back to her. She placed it back inside and then rang the bell with her usual enthusiasm. Unfortunately, the cockle flew out, which startled Banana into dropping the bell onto the floor, causing it to smash into smithereens. She stared in horror at the shattered pieces all over the floor, causing us all to burst out laughing.

'Stop laughing! Why are you laughing? Stop laughing, you bastards!' Banana always said the word 'bastard' with more venom than anyone we had ever known.

'We're telling General and the kids. What a charming way to treat their present!'

'No, don't tell him, please,' begged the ever-dramatic Banana.

The following Saturday, Big Mark and Malcolm went down

the high street and bought her a new, bigger bell, which we all chipped in for. We presented it to her for her birthday that night, while playing 'Ring My Bell' by Anita Ward.

I used to let some of the foreign girls come behind the bar and ring the bell for 'last orders', as they had no such practice in their countries, probably because, in Spain, Germany, France and most other countries in Europe, they could drink as late as they want anyway.

Steve and Harry used to pull me up about that, and also on the fact that, despite having the strict rule in force that only paying customers could use the toilets, whenever a nice girl came in and asked, the rule was overlooked.

'She asked really politely, though!' I would argue in my defence.

'Nothing to do with the fact that she was really fit, then?' Steve would ask.

'That's nothing to do with it!'

'So how comes, then, whenever a bloke comes in, he's told that he has to buy something?' Harry pointed out.

'It's the way they ask,' I protested.

'You fuckin' liar!'

Banana often made us laugh with her comments. Although she spoke very good English, she would come out with her own unique phrases, such as 'I have no fancy' when she did not feel like doing something. One customer asked what home-cooked meals we had available, to which she replied, 'Ah, we have Shepherd's Bush Pie!'

She spoke a sort of Cockney/Italian dialect and would switch between the two, and I realised how well her English was coming on after hearing her yelling at Dennis, 'Shut your chops, Dennis, or I'll give you a knuckle sandwich!'

There was one occasion when a young bloke came barging into the café.

'Can I help you?' Banana asked him.

'I'm just using your toilet,' he told her, with an obvious lack of manners.

'You have to buy something if you want to use the toilet,' Banana informed him. This might seem mean, but we had to tighten up dramatically, as we had half the population of Hounslow coming in to use our toilets. We did not mind if somebody asked politely, but we would stop them when they attempted to march in there.

'I don't want to buy anything; I just want to go to the toilet,' he protested stroppily.

'Look, you can buy something for ten pence here,' explained Banana.

'Oh, fuck it, then!' the bloke shouted, turning to go out of the door.

'No, you fuck off!' Banana screamed at him.

I was chatting to a mate, Dapo, and we immediately jumped out of our seats.

'What's going on?' Dapo demanded to know.

'I didn't say "fuck off"; I said "fuck it, then",' the irate youngster explained, before going out of the door, almost in tears.

Gordon was an old, well-spoken, well-educated man who used to come in every Wednesday at 1 p.m., as regular as clockwork. He always liked to have his dinner with a glass of water and then his pudding with a cup of tea. He would eat in total silence, but, the moment he finished the last mouthful, he would burst into life and start quizzing everyone in the café. He had an amazing all-round knowledge, and we always commented on how he would have made a fantastic teacher because he made every subject interesting.

Ted's son, Martin, was Banana's best customer. Fortunately, he was not a regular in the pub at the time of Eleanor's wind-up, or General might have ended up giving him a ticking-off in the corridor as well! Martin would run around, doing errands for Banana just to keep in her good books. He did not speak to Billy for ages when he thought he was trying to edge in as Banana's favourite errand boy, but he need not have worried, as Billy carried these tasks out for her under duress!

Anybody who upset Banana would appear on the 'Board of Shame'. Richard's name was almost a permanent fixture on it, as he kept disappearing without paying for his tea. Ged's name would also regularly appear on there for not paying for his ticket whenever we had a live band.

'I shan't be 'ere long, as I've got work in t' morning,' he would claim, when Ivor or I were trying to get him to pay up. Then, about three hours later, Ged would be up on the dance floor, doing a John Travolta!

After the bomb explosions on 7/07, Richard came in for a cup of tea before heading off for work at Paddington Underground Station.

'Richard, there's no tubes running and no buses in the centre,' Phil, sitting at the bar with his Courage Best, warned him.

'I don't care. I've spoken to them at work and they told me that they need me in, so I'm going even if I have to walk all the way there!' he shouted, as he marched out of the door with a 'Blitz-like' spirit.

'Oi, you lot, Richard's gone off to save London, but he still didn't pay for his cup of tea!' I pointed out to the others.

Later that day, there was a sombre mood in the pub, as the day's events became clearer. We were worried about Ged, who drove a bus out of King's Cross Garage every day. We discussed how, besides the bastards who put the explosives on the buses, everyone's life was decided by fate.

'Ged could go and buy a packet of fags, and those few seconds could mean him getting caught in the blast,' Malcolm suggested.

We all looked at each other. 'No, that would never happen. Ged would never buy any fags!' we all agreed.

The Three Masons

There was a group of notorious brothers in the area, who I shall call the Nortons. There had only ever been one incident involving any of them in our pub, and that had been in our first few months, when one – I shall call him Roy Norton – poked a bloke called Pat in the eye. Apart from that incident, they had not caused any trouble. However, we felt we had to bar them, as we could sense it would only be a matter of time before they did.

Several months later, I came in the back way and noticed Roy Norton standing at the bar.

'Is it all right if I have a drink, then?' he asked.

'No, you can't,' I replied.

'Why the fuck not?' he demanded to know.

'You know why not. Let's not go down that road again.'

'Look, I can bring a right firm down here,' he threatened. 'I can bring Paul Powell down here with me. What do you think about that?'

Paul Powell's name rang a bell. He had been in the year below me at school and, by all accounts, he was a raving lunatic who had spent 95 per cent of his time since leaving school inside. He was described as 'institutionalised'.

'How far are you prepared to go?' he asked me.

'As far as I have to,' I replied. 'It's my pub and I'm not going anywhere.'

'I've got a shooter in the motor!' he threatened.

'You don't scare me,' I insisted, as he stared at me continuously.

'Yeah, I know I don't,' he agreed, appearing to relax a little. However, he was soon off again.

'Look, your mates, the Bassetts don't run Hounslow, and neither does Malloy. No, they don't! I'll tell you who runs Hounslow,' he ranted.

'Who does, then?' I asked, interested in what was coming next.

'I'll tell you who!' he shouted. 'The fuckin' Freemasons, that's who! Yeah, that's right, your fuckin' mates the Bassetts don't run Hounslow; the Freemasons do!' He continued yelling as he walked towards the exit. Everyone in the pub had heard what he was shouting.

The next day, Steve Bassett came into the pub and ushered me to one side.

'I hear Roy Norton was in here slagging us off yesterday. What was he saying?'

'He was saying that your family doesn't run Hounslow and neither do the Malloys, but the Freemasons do,' I revealed.

'The cheeky bastard! We'll see about that. I'm off to see my brothers now, and you wait and see what happens!' He stormed out of the pub, absolutely livid about what had been said.

The next day, I was behind the bar when Steve came in and ushered me aside once again.

'You know what we were talking about yesterday?'

'Yeah, of course,' I replied.

'Well, neither my brothers nor me have ever heard of these brothers, the Masons,' he told me.

'Who?' I asked, not having a clue what he was talking about.

'You know, what Norton was on about the other day when he was going on about those three brothers, the Masons, who run Hounslow,' he explained.

'Oh, them!' I exclaimed, fighting to keep a straight face.

When we discussed it afterwards, we had visions of Steve and his brothers going from pub to pub, searching for these 'Mason Brothers' who were challenging their authority!

An Unwelcome Visitor

A couple of months later, I was playing pool in the public bar with Rab and Gurmit when Orlaigh, our barmaid, called me over.

'Do you recognise that big bloke leaning on the post through there?'

I looked through to the other bar and could see a bloke with short, cropped blond hair, leaning on one of the brass poles at the bar. He had trouble written all over him.

'No. Why's that, then?'

'Because he's having a right go at John and Ron,' explained Orlaigh.

'Well, I think he's about to come unstuck, then,' I replied, as John was an ex-Scots Guard and built like Mike Tyson, and Ron had spent years in the Merchant Navy and, although he was in his sixties, could still more than look after himself.

'I'm not so sure,' responded Orlaigh. She was from Northern Ireland and was very streetwise, so, when she gave that response, it made me take the situation seriously. I went through to have a closer look.

'You fuckin' wanker!' the man was shouting at John, who, surprisingly, was keeping his cool. 'I'll fuckin' give you some, you fuckin' Scottish bastard!'

'Excuse me, do you mind keeping it down a bit?' I interrupted.

His head shot round and, with his eyes blazing, he yelled at me. 'Why; who the fuck are you?'

'I'm the landlord.'

'I don't give a fuck!' he shouted. 'What the fuck are you gonna do about it?'

Here we go; I've got a right one here! I thought to myself, although, I have to admit, I could feel my heart beating faster, as he seemed like a right lunatic. I lifted the bar flap so that I could go and deal with this maniac, but no sooner had I lifted it up than he was there in front of me, ready for a confrontation. I usually had to go right up to where the trouble was, but, in this case, it had come right to me.

'So, what yer gonna do now, then?' he demanded to know.

I sized up the situation for what seemed like an eternity. He had a pint glass in his hand and was holding it in such a way that I was in no doubt that he would have got a great deal of pleasure out of sticking it straight into my face.

For the first time, I became aware that he was not alone but had an accomplice with him. He was a small bloke from an Indian background, who spoke with a Cockney accent. He edged up to me and whispered in my ear.

'Look, mate: don't provoke him whatever you do. He's an absolute psycho. He's just come out from a long stretch and he's ready to explode. Look, let us finish our drinks and I'll try and get him out without a scene.'

The music had stopped, and I was aware that everybody was watching the situation in nervous anticipation and listening to every word. It is always worse when there is a deadly silence in the background. I was also aware that there were some middle-aged women in the pub, including Patricia and Christine, so his friend's suggestion seemed the best idea.

'OK, mate; if you can do it, that'd be great.'

'You fuckin' wanker! I knew you were a bottle job!' the blond screamed at me.

'Right, I've had enough now; drink up and go!' I replied.

'Bollocks, you tosser! I've paid for these drinks, so you can pay for them if you want us to go,' he insisted.

I fished a five-pound note out of my pocket and he made a grab for it. I pulled my hand away.

'You ain't havin' it. I'll give it to your mate, but I ain't giving it to you.'

This may appear petty, but in this situation you are in a psychological battle as well, and I did not want this man thinking that I would do whatever he wanted.

'I still ain't fuckin' leaving!' he shouted.

I did not know how much longer I could keep my temper, but his mate was once again whispering anxiously in my ear.

'Please, mate, let him finish his drink and I'll bring the money in tomorrow.' He turned to his friend. 'Come on, Paul; let's go now, mate,' he attempted to coax him.

'Don't you fuckin' touch me!' the nutter, who I now knew to be called Paul, yelled angrily.

'Oh, that's great, Paul: you wanna start on me now!' his friend shouted at him.

Powell slammed his glass down on the table and started rifling through his pockets. Scottish John seized the opportunity to come over, he removed Paul's glass from the table and took it to the bar.

'Tip that down the sink,' John instructed Orlaigh.

'Oi, where's my drink fuckin' gone?' Paul screamed. He turned round just in time to see his beer disappearing down the sink. He erupted in fury.

'Oi, you Scottish bastard, that's my fuckin' beer!' he ranted, charging at John, before punching him full-force in the face. John did not even flinch, which, taking into consideration the fact that this nutter was well over six foot and probably about sixteen stone, was amazing. I think that Paul was shocked as well, so he lashed out with another free punch in the face. To my amazement, John did not react at all, but I had by now had enough of this bastard. I ran and jumped at him, causing us both to crash to the floor. He landed on top of me, but I somehow managed to turn the tables and was suddenly on top of him. I got in a few punches before he lifted his hands in what appeared to be a signal that he had had enough. Some regulars pulled me off him, but, as soon as he was on his feet, he charged at John again, punching him in the face for the third time. However, this time, John did hit him back, and within a matter of seconds they were both on the floor, with John pummelling Paul as he held him in a 'Big Daddy grip'. I joined them down there, and Paul's blond hair quickly became claret. The regulars pulled us off, with Gurmit's calm manner persuading a reluctant John to let go. Gurmit could always calm anyone down in those sorts of situations.

'Come on, Paul; let's get out of here. The Old Bill are coming!' shouted Paul's mate, and with that they rushed towards the exit, only for Paul to stop, turn around and pick up a bar stool, which he launched like an Exocet missile. It rebounded off a beam and hit John straight in the face, breaking his cheekbone. It definitely had not been John's night!

It was only after the incident was over that I discovered that the man was Paul Powell, the same bloke that Roy Norton had threatened me with. At school, his hair had been auburn, and he was obviously much bigger and stockier than when I had known him at school. I do not think that he recognised me either, although I am not sure that would have made that much difference to him.

John and I went through some grief together at the pub, but we have stood up for each other when the chips were down. On one occasion, an African bloke was shouting at Cissie, an African girl who used to be a regular in the pub.

'These fuckin' people don't care about you! You know what they're like.'

'They do; they're my friends in here,' replied Cissie.

'These bastards here! You know what white people are like!' he continued.

'Excuse me, do you mind keeping it down a bit?' I asked him.

'Look, I'm talking to her. It's none of your business.'

'It is my business, 'cause you're shouting so the whole pub can hear you. It's also offensive, what you're shouting, so cut it out.'

I went and sat down, but within a few minutes he was off again.

'Are you OK, Cissie?' I enquired, although it was plain to see that she was in distress.

'No, I'm not.'

'OK, mate, time to go,' I said, and with that he stood up and squared up to me, or, rather, he squared down to me, as he must have been at least six-foot-five. In normal circumstances, I would have done what my grandad used to advise me to do, 'get the first one in,' but, being the landlord, I always preferred getting them out without any trouble if possible.

Suddenly, John appeared from nowhere and started shoving the man towards the exit. Within five seconds, he was standing out in the street, glaring at me.

'I see. You Irishman get this big Englishman to do your dirty work for you!'

He had got it wrong about both of us. All four of my grandparents were English, and John was not very impressed with the man's assumption.

'What did yer fuckin' say?' John growled, with such venom that the African looked startled, 'I'm not English, do yer understand? I'm Scottish, not English!' John fumed as the man quickly disappeared.

Despite John being a proud Scotsman, he did not hold back from sorting out his fellow Scots if he felt it was necessary. He had bust-ups with Duncan and Richard, as well as a major one with an ex-Scots Guard called Billy, who was about six-foot-five. Billy was, on the whole, a decent bloke, although, by his own admission, he could sometimes get out of hand. One Sunday night, he started having a go at John, who was having a drink with his wife, Helena.

'And yer won't fuckin' come outside with me because you know you'd fuckin' lose!' Billy shouted, before slamming his glass down on John's table and storming off to the toilet.

John sat there for a few seconds, then got up and followed Billy into the toilet, where he gave him a good hiding. Billy took it well though, and was man enough to admit that he had started it, and that John had taught him a lesson.

'Could yer ask John if he could give me my earring back, as it was a present from my missus?' he asked me, as I gave him a cloth to wipe the blood from his ear. 'And could he also give me back the part of my ear that's attached to it?' he added, with a wry smile.

The Sandwich Eater

In the majority of cases, the tough blokes cause no problems and know how to behave. Sometimes, trouble can come from the most surprising people. There was one man called Alex, who was aged about fifty. He was a miserable, dour Scot, who was always smartly dressed but was rude and unsociable.

One Wednesday evening, I was asking the questions on a Quiz Night and, as usual, Alex refused to join in. However, he was not so slow in stuffing his face with the sandwiches we provided on these occasions. I was just starting the music round when I had to go into the public bar to calm down a couple of customers who were arguing. I was in the middle of doing this when the door opened and in walked Alex. This surprised me, as he was a creature of habit and had never been in that bar before. He would come in, buy his pint of Guinness and sit on his own, reading his newspaper, only looking up every now and again to give someone a dirty look. What was an even bigger surprise to me was the fact that he came straight over and had a right go at me. I had a job understanding what his grievance was at first, but it translated to something like this: 'What sort of a Mickey Mouse pub are you running here, when the dregs of society are free to come in and help themselves to sandwiches every Wednesday?'

'You're being a bit harsh on yourself, aren't you, Alex?' I replied cheekily.

Unsurprisingly, it did not go down very well!

'You're a fucking wanker who couldn't run a piss-up in a brewery!' he concluded, before storming out the back door. I followed him out there, as I was curious as to what had brought on his outburst.

'What did you say?'

'I said that you are a fucking wanker. That Denton comes in and helps himself to sandwiches without ever joining in the quiz,' he yelled, almost frothing at the mouth.

'So do you, Alex, and you never join in the quiz.'

'You bastard, I'm never coming here again.'

'Good; fuck off, then!' I replied, finally losing patience with him.

I felt no threat whatsoever, as he did not seem like your typical yob. I had just turned to go back into the pub when I felt a glancing blow to the side of the face. I was shocked and a bit embarrassed, but, when he followed up by punching me in the mouth, I knew that I had to defend myself. After a short while, some of the others came out to break it up.

Afterwards, there was the usual post-incident inquest in which everyone had their say. Banana asked me to explain what had happened, as she could not speak or understand much English at that time. After I had described the events, she looked at me and then commented enthusiastically, 'I understand, Chris: he hit you because he didn't like the sandwiches!'

'That's right, Banana!' I agreed, smiling.

Some Other Characters

Scouse John was actually from Birkenhead, so he was not a real Scouser and, in fact, regularly broadcast this, especially in the presence of true Scousers, such as Steve and Harry. General and I would often wind him up, claiming that either Steve or Harry had called him a Woollyback Poofter, which would really get him going.

John looked identical to the Proclaimers. It would be interesting to know whether John's dad visited Scotland many years ago!

He was a great dancer, probably the second best in the pub after Kirpal. Mind you, Tony Coombes was top boy as far as Ska was concerned, and Scottish John and Malcolm did a great dance to 'Lip Up Fatty' that Buster Bloodvessel himself or Nobby would have been proud of! John and Mal were Shrek lookalikes and used to wind people up that they were twins. Their only problem was that Malcolm spoke with a Cockney accent and John with a strong Glaswegian one. 'Our parents split up when we were eleven, so our dad brought me up in Glasgow, and our mum brought Mal up in London', John would explain.

They were quite a partnership, especially if there was the possibility of trouble. However, there was one occasion when they were both well out of their depth, causing them to back away and admit defeat. Malcolm had decided to get the Hoover out. 'John, give us an 'and with this thing', he called out, after failing to get it going. John was always happy to back Malcolm up, but this was a case of the blind leading the blind, as neither of them had a clue. They stood there, scratching their heads, looking at it as if it were a UFO. Housework, it appeared, was not one of their strong points, and as John once pointed out, 'I don't do kitchens'.

Woollyback John and his wife, Ruth, had their wedding reception in the Cambridge, and what a great day it was! Everyone had started drinking at midday, but, because there was such a great spread there, people were constantly eating, so nobody was too drunk. By 3 a.m., everyone had gone home except for John and Ruth, the bride and groom! I think that they just did not want their special day to end.

We had to have a word with John on a few occasions, as, after a few pints, he would sometimes suddenly change and start being abusive to other customers. However, we had to laugh on one occasion at his rudeness. A blind man, who could be quite obnoxious, used to frequent the pub, accompanied by a small Indian woman, who was only about four-foot-six. When the man came up to the bar one day, John turned around and made conversation with the man. The trouble was that John had by then started his sixth pint, so he was beginning to get a bit obstreperous.

'Your missus has been lying to you.'

'What do you mean, she's been lying to me?' the blind man asked John.

'She's tricked you. She told you she was six foot with blonde hair and blue eyes!'

There was a regular called Christine, who was in her fifties. She used to come in every night and order two Bells in separate glasses, each with a slice of lemon, and two bottles of ginger ale. After pouring the bottles of ginger ale into the two drinks, she would then take alternate mouthfuls out of each glass.

'Why do you do that, Christine?' Livi asked her one day, when his curiosity got the better of him.

'My husband always drank Bells with a slice of lemon and ginger ale, so when I come in the pub, I get one for me and one for him.'

That was a touching story, but, because of the way she behaved sometimes, I began to doubt whether she had ever really had a husband.

The first year she drank in the pub, she celebrated her birthday in February, and then, in September, she claimed it was her birthday again.

'I'm sure she's had a birthday already this year,' remarked General.

'Yeah, I was thinking that as well,' I agreed.

However, we went ahead and got her a card and bought her

and her dead husband a drink. We also got her a cake and sang 'Happy Birthday', as we did with all the regulars.

We started to suspect that she had a vivid imagination when, every couple of weeks, she would come in and announce that somebody else in her family had died. She must have lost five sisters and four brothers in the space of three months, but it got beyond a joke when her mum died for the second time in a year.

February came again and Christine came in, announcing that it was her birthday. We accepted this, as we remembered that her 'first birthday' the previous year had been in February. However, this time General marked it in the diary.

September soon came round, and Christine, true to form, came in one evening all dressed up. Although it was amusing it, still cheesed us off a bit that she was trying to con drinks and a cake off us. This particular night, I was not in a very good mood. I did not wish her 'Happy Birthday', as I was not prepared to go through all that rubbish again.

'Hello, Christine; your usual?' I asked her.

'Yes, please,' she replied, in her strict voice.

I served her the usual two Bells with lemon and two ginger ales and then held out my hand for the money as she stood there, motionless. We stood there, looking at each other, for what seemed like ages.

'Aren't you getting them for my birthday?' she demanded to know.

'No, Christine, only the Queen gets away with having two birthdays in one year,' I replied.

'But it's my birthday today!' she insisted.

'No, it's not. Your birthday is in February,' I argued.

Everybody was looking at me as if I were Scrooge, so I decided to prove it. I grabbed the diary and turned the pages back to February, where General had written Christine's name.

'There you are. That's when your birthday is!' I announced triumphantly.

She burst into tears and began rifling through her handbag for, I assumed, a handkerchief. However, she pulled out her birth certificate.

'Now do you believe me?' she asked tearfully.

I looked at the birth certificate, which confirmed that it was indeed her birthday. She had been telling the truth, and I was the heartless one who had made her cry on her birthday. What the customers did not know was that she had totally lied about her birthday in February, not to mention the February before as well. I bit my tongue and bought her and her late husband a drink, but drew the line as far as buying her a cake was concerned.

Christine was always claiming that someone or other had told her to 'fuck off' in the street or on the bus. One day, she came in, crying. I assumed that somebody else had 'died'. She had run out of brothers and sisters dying and had recently started on her nephews and nieces. The other regulars were all making a fuss of her, which was what she thrived on.

'Chris, will you go and reassure Christine, as she thinks she's barred from here?' Scottish John asked me.

'As if she would have been barred from here,' I commented impatiently.

'What's up, Christine?' I asked.

'She thinks she's been barred and she's all upset,' explained Livi.

'Of course she's not barred,' I said.

'I am!' she insisted. 'I came here last night and, as I walked to the door, this man told me to fuck off and said that I was barred.'

'Christine, if we were going to bar you, we would tell you ourselves,' I snapped, before walking back behind the bar, ignoring the remainder of the conversation. They might have thought I was being insensitive, but we had to deal with this sort of rubbish all the time. Half of the things said in the pub were simply not true.

One of her funnier stories was after the Paul Powell incident, when she tearfully told anyone who would listen that Powell had told her to fuck off before throwing the stool at her, only to miss and hit John instead!

Tony Baloney was great fun, especially when doing his Mick Jagger impression with Ralph to 'Tumbling Dice'. He was always chasing the women, so General claimed he was on a round-the-world cruise with a woman in every port. On a couple of occasions, he came into the pub with a lady called Audrienne, who used to be in the Marvelettes. She grabbed the microphone to sing for about an hour and was absolutely fantastic. We found it fascinating when she described how she still felt tremendous bitterness towards Diana Ross even after all those years.

'The Supremes were suddenly given all the best songs and promoted as the top all-girl Motown band just because Diana Ross was shagging Berry Gordy,' she claimed. Berry Gordy, Jr was, of course, the boss of Tamla Motown.

On another occasion, she and Tony could not keep their hands off each other while propped against the bar. Tiziana promptly leant over and drew imaginary curtains around them. I do not think that Tony knew what was going on, although Audrienne found it hilarious.

Tony stayed above the pub for a while and, although it was big, we were amazed that, over a month after moving in, he was still getting lost upstairs. However, we had our suspicions that it was not completely genuine after locking up one night and going upstairs to hear Tony calling out 'sorry, wrong room' after bursting into Maria's room.

'What are you up to, Tony?' I asked jokingly.

'I was looking for the bathroom,' he said.

'But, Tony, the bathroom's next to your room!'

'I know, but I got lost!' he claimed, grinning rather sheepishly.

He used to tell Banana a poem, which he claimed he had made up especially for her:

'A sea of serenity,

An ocean of love,

An island of tranquillity,

The peace of a dove.'

Then, one night, while we were having a late drink, Tony disappeared into the corridor to talk on his mobile. After a few minutes, Banana went out there to go to the ladies' and heard Tony uttering 'her poem' down his mobile to an American woman! He was in a lot of trouble for that!

That American woman told Tony how excited her postman had got when he was delivering a letter Tony had sent her. He had written his address on the back of the envelope, and the postman had noticed it and ran up her drive, shouting at the top of his voice,

'You've got a letter from the Duke of Cambridge, England!'

Audrienne was not the only celebrity in the pub. Jimi Hendrix played his first UK gig in the Cambridge, although that was many years before we took over. Livi remembered it, although, as he explained, 'He was just a long-haired bloke who came in here with his band and made a lot of noise up on stage, but, of course, this was before he was famous.'

Freddie Mercury and Phil Collins were rumoured to have performed there as well, and there could be some truth in this as they both came from the area. Freddie came from Feltham, a couple of miles up the road, and could not have been more different to the average bloke from there!

Eddie, a regular for many years and a drinking partner of Ken and Dennis, claimed to have been in the Real Thing, a band famous for a string of hits in the seventies. He moved back up to Liverpool just before we left the pub.

Scrabble Dave's brother, Rex Brayley, who played lead guitar in Love Affair, best known for their number one hit, 'Everlasting Love,' used to come in with Dave occasionally. Dave was also a useful drummer.

There was also Rick Kerr, who claimed he was with Marmalade, which had a number one with a cover of The Beatles 'Ob-La-Di, Ob-La-Da' as well as other big-selling hits.

We could have had a real talent night if we had got all of the above together on stage, but, unfortunately, the best we managed was Livi, Harry, Tony Baloney, Darren – my mate, the bus driver – and I having a jamming session! Darren could play it well, and so could Livi until he had an accident at work in which he lost the tip of his finger.

Dave was known as Scrabble Dave for the simple reason that he used to come in several times a week to play Scrabble. He was an alcoholic who managed to give up the drink; he would still come into the pub to see us all and to play Scrabble, but would always stick to J20s. Everyone was really impressed with how he had managed to turn his life around.

One night, we organised a residents' meeting in the pub, where General, Maria, Banana, Finnigan, Tony and I would discuss various issues.

'The one thing that really gets up my nose is the smell of kippers in the morning,' Maria commented.

'Who's responsible for that smell, then?' asked Banana.

'Oh, sorry, guys, that's me,' Tony confessed. 'In future, I'll try not to cook them so early in the morning.'

'There's somebody falling asleep and leaving their radio on all night, and it's keeping the kids awake,' General chimed in, with a deadly serious face.

'Well... er, sorry, guys, I'm afraid that's me again,' revealed an embarrassed Tony.

What he did not know was that it was a wind-up and we had thought of everything we could blame him for. It was incredible how he fell for it even when we got up to the twentieth point on the list. Finnigan kept reassuring him by saying, 'It's not a witch-hunt, Tony!'

'I know, guys. I'll try not to do that any more,' Tony replied, sounding like Neil in *The Young Ones*.

One night, all of us who were living upstairs happened to be down in the bar, having a late drink. Ralph was the only other person there, and he was demanding to be let out so that he could catch the last bus home. After we let him out, we all went upstairs, where the other five went into each bedroom while I went into the bathroom. We were all waiting for Ralph's bus to pull up, then, one by one, we opened each window and leant out to shout at the top of our voices, 'Good night, Ralph!' It was like a scene from *The Waltons*, and the bus driver found it funnier than Ralph did!

On Finnigan's birthday, we all went downstairs for a drink. Finnigan was always supplying the rest of us with milk, so the five of us decided to buy him milk for his birthday in size order. Maria, who was the smallest, wrapped up a sachet; General gave him one pint; I bought him two pints, Banana four pints and Tony bought him six pints. We wrapped them all up individually and presented them all to Finny in the pub. He started unwrapping them and he guessed the joke after the third one. He had enough milk to keep us going for a week.

One Saturday night, I was upstairs with Banana and our dog, Duke, and was about to go down to start playing the music. Duke did not seem too happy about it and started whining.

'Come on, Duke, don't be a silly boy; I've got to go downstairs,' I insisted.

He continued howling, so I finally lost patience.

'Here you are, Tiziana: hold him; he's being silly.'

'Come on, darling, I'll look after you!' she said, hugging Duke tightly.

I leant over to give him a kiss just as Banana gave him a tight squeeze, and – *whoosh* – it was like I had been squirted in the face with a water pistol. However, this was not water! Duke had been trying to tell us all along that he had been bursting to go to the toilet, only for Banana to give him a tight squeeze just as I happened to be directly in the firing line. I ran into the bathroom and washed my face, then burst out laughing when I saw Banana trying to keep a straight face!

Poor old Banana; when she first moved above the pub, she would be preparing dinner when suddenly her bowl of salad or vegetables would disappear and then, after she had spent ten minutes looking for it, would reappear in a different place. We played these tricks for months before she finally realised what was going on. She must have thought she was losing her marbles.

On one occasion, when I was planning to hide something of hers, I was hiding in the corridor leading to the kitchen, waiting for my chance, as she took the chicken she was cooking out of the oven. She put it down, peeled back some of the foil and looked at her masterpiece with real satisfaction before leaning forward and smelling it.

'Ah, lov-er-ly jubb-er-ly!' she exclaimed, rubbing her hands in anticipation of the great feast she was about to enjoy.

I burst out laughing, so that was one occasion on which I was unable to hide anything, although I would have loved to have hidden that chicken from her!

Federico the Mad Italian

One Friday in June 2000, two months after taking over, I was behind the bar, having a chat with my cousin Maxine, who had popped in. An Italian bloke was at the bar and appeared very sociable.

'Where are you from?' I asked.

'Milano,' he replied.

'What are you doing here, then?' asked Maxine.

'I'm over for a friend's wedding. Actually, it's my ex-girlfriend's wedding,' he explained. 'And you are very beautiful!' he added.

'Thank you!'

'What is your name?'

'Maxine.'

'Ah, Max-ine; such a lovely name! I am Federico,' he announced.

'When is the wedding?' Maxine asked him.

'I'm going to Bristol this evening to stay with my ex-girlfriend, as she's getting married tomorrow,' he explained, as if that were perfectly normal. Maybe it is in Milan and Bristol!

'So what are you doing in here?' I asked.

'I was on the Underground and decided to get off at Hounslow East, and this was the first pub I came to.'

We had not been recommended in Milan, then!

We had a good laugh for a couple of hours, until he got up to leave for Bristol.

'I will definitely come and see you again!' he promised.

He kept his promise, because, about three months later, he entered the pub with a big grin on his face. He ordered the drink that the person next to him was drinking. This was a real trait of his, but the problem would be when, during the course of an evening, he would have a chat with nine or ten different people, so he would end up drinking nine or ten different beers.

The following day, I was going over to Richmond Park to take Michael and Michelle's dog, Molly, for a walk, and asked Federico whether he wanted to come. My friend, Monica, from Sardinia, worked in an ice cream van in the park at the time, and I wanted to play a joke on her. I dug out a photo of myself and explained to Federico on the way there what I wanted him to do. We arrived near the van where she worked, and I stayed with Molly behind the trees nearby while Federico approached her.

'Ciao,' Federico greeted her.

'Ciao; can I help you?' asked Monica.

'I hope so. I work for Interpol and I am here in London trying to find the owner of a pub called the Duke of Cambridge. His name is Christopher Pitts, and this is a photo of him. Do you know this man?'

Poor Monica stared at Federico in shock and then at the photo, but did not say a word.

'Do you know anyone by that name or anyone who has got a pub in Hounslow?' he asked her.

'No, I don't,' replied Monica.

'Are you absolutely sure? He is a very dangerous criminal and we need to find him.'

'I've told you, I don't know him,' Monica repeated firmly. I was really proud of her loyalty and, in fact, I felt really guilty when I stepped out from behind the tree to interrupt the investigation!

That evening, we saw the first instance of the darker side of Federico's personality. There was a crowd of us at the end of the bar, having a drink and enjoying the music, when, suddenly, Aisha screamed, 'Give me my fuckin' drink back now!'

'No; you've had too much to drink already,' he insisted.

She was a tough Glaswegian and was not going to take that. 'I think that I'll be the judge of that.'

'It's not right for girls to drink so much,' he lectured her, with the utmost belief in what he was saying.

'I'll drink as much as I like, thank you very much!' Aisha shouted, as she sent Federico flying with a shove and grabbed her drink back in one movement. She gulped it straight down.

'A double vodka, please,' she called out to Carmel as Federico sat there, looking like a wounded animal.

There was a group of very nice foreign girls who used to come into the pub. Amongst them were Jennifer, a French girl, and an Italian girl called Antonella (*è molto bella!*).

'Which one do you fancy, Chris?' Scouse Steve asked me.

'All of them!' I replied, truthfully.

Federico was not keen on them, as they had, unlike the English girls in the pub, not paid him any special attention, although they had been polite to him.

'They are all slags!' he chimed in.

'What was that?' I asked.

'They are all slags!' he repeated.

'You don't even know them,' I protested.

'It doesn't matter; they are,' he insisted.

'You fuckin' idiot. Just 'cause they haven't paid you any attention.'

'Leave him alone; he's entitled to his opinion,' two girls, who were really mouthy, said.

'You mind your own business!' I retorted.

Federico apologised the next day and was all right for the next few months until Rab's daughter, Caroline, started bringing her mate Charlotte into the pub. She was an attractive blonde girl, who Federico fell for immediately. Charlotte enjoyed the attention at first, as she was only nineteen, but it got too much when Federico began escorting her to the toilet and standing guard outside. He started ignoring Stuart the barman and me, and things got worse when he started glaring at us while shouting in Italian. He had really lost the plot. One night, he went too far, causing Stuart to wrestle him to the ground, threatening to sort him out in the car park.

He came in about a year later to tell me that he was going back to Milan.

'What happened to you, Federico? You went really strange?'

'I know I behaved badly, Chris, but I can't help it. Girls make me go crazy!'

As I pointed out, Federico was a raving lunatic, but he could be really funny as well. One thing he introduced into the pub was calling everyone by the Italian translation of their name. We had Marco, Ricardo, Raymondo, Stefano, Franco, Rolando and so on.

Harry thought he was safe, until Federico started addressing him as 'Oragano'!

Stuart was feeling a bit left out. 'What about me, Freddie?' he asked.

Federico looked at Stuart for what seemed like ages, and then shouted, 'Eduardo!'

'Eduardo?' Stuart repeated in astonishment.

'But Ted's Eduardo,' I protested.

'It doesn't matter,' Federico responded. 'Stuart can be Eduardo as well!'

I began calling Harry 'Oragano' as well, and then, for no reason apart from the fact that I was once with an Italian girl whose surname was Esposito, began calling him 'Oragano Esposito'. One day, Harry was in the pub and I shouted out 'Oragano Esposito', which just had a nice ring to it.

'What does that mean?' Harry asked me.

'I've no idea,' I replied.

'Fred, what does Esposito mean?' Harry asked Federico.

'It means "one who exposes himself",' explained Federico. That explains the term 'Flash Harry', then!

One evening my mum and dad were in the bar, having a drink, when my mum commented to Federico. 'I'd love to know how to make pasta properly.'

'Don't worry; I can show you,' Federico assured her.

'That would be lovely!' my mum replied enthusiastically.

They arranged to meet the next day, so that he could show her.

'But have you got everything you need here?' my mum asked, a bit sceptical, as she had seen Federico's food larder, which consisted of twenty cans of baked beans and spaghetti (the tinned variety).

'Of course I have; don't worry,' he reassured her.

He came out of the larder with a carrier bag, filled a pan with water, added some salt and put it on the hob. We watched with amazement as he pulled a packet of pasta from out of the bag and poured the contents into the saucepan. Much to Federico's surprise, we started laughing.

'What is so funny?' he demanded to know.

'We know how to cook pasta like that, Federico. We thought you were going to show us the proper way to make it!' my mum explained.

One night, I was awoken by somebody banging on my bedroom door.

'Chris, there's a funny noise coming from downstairs!' Federico whispered nervously.

I walked into the corridor and realised that the 'funny noise' he referred to was the alarm.

'Shit, some bastards are breaking in!' I mumbled to myself, still half-asleep.

I hurried into the kitchen, grabbed one of the kitchen knives that Fitzy had confiscated from the 'Tamil Tiger' and crept downstairs. I opened the downstairs door as quietly as possible, as I wanted to surprise them. I crept all around the pub, my eyes straining to see in the dark, but to no avail.

They must be down in the cellar, I thought to myself as I crept down the wooden stairs, hoping that the noise of the alarm ringing would drown out the sound of the creaking floorboards.

I was suddenly aware of somebody following me. I turned around abruptly, only to be looking up at a tall, dark figure holding a knife similar to the one I was holding. I lost my footing and fell back down the remaining half-a-dozen steps, landing awkwardly in the process. I gripped the knife in anticipation, but the intruder had stopped.

'Chris, are you OK?' I could not see him, but there was no mistaking that Italian accent of his.

'Shit! Federico, is that you? What the fuck are you doing?' I demanded to know.

'I thought you might need some help!' he explained.

'Oh, OK. Well, thanks very much!' I replied, struggling to show my appreciation!

Hurricane Rita

We took on an eighteen-year-old Finnish girl in the café as Tiziana's assistant. In Finland, where there are loads of beautiful girls, I am sure that she would not be deemed as anything special, so she probably could not believe her luck when the punters in the Duke treated her like a princess. The attention she received, as with a few of the barmaids we had, went straight to her head. Mathew and Jimmy, who were mates at the time, had a bet to see who could get hold of her first. Mathew won, but only just, as she took Jimmy over the same park half an hour later and shagged him as well!

A few nights later, when we were sitting upstairs, we could hear Jimmy shouting 'Rita' from the street. He used to call her name in a comical, high-pitched tone, so we knew instantly that it was him.

'Go and listen and find out what they're up to,' Tiziana instructed, out of sheer curiosity (or nosiness!).

I sneaked into the bathroom without turning the light on and could hear Jimmy even clearer.

'Rita! Are you awake?'

I popped my head out of the bathroom window, expecting Jimmy to be standing directly under Rita's room, but, to my horror, he was looking straight up at the window where my head had just appeared.

'Oh, there you are!' he exclaimed excitedly. 'I thought that was your room! Any chance of coming up?'

I was speechless. I knew that I had put on some weight through excessive beer-drinking, but nevertheless was still shocked at the speed in which I had turned into a buxom blonde!

I still did not respond and was considering a tactical withdrawal when Jimmy's eyes adjusted.

'Oh, shit! Chris, is that you?' he stammered. 'W-what one's R-Rita's room, then?'

'That one there,' I replied, as embarrassed as Jimmy.

'Well, what happened, then?' Banana demanded to know when I returned.

Not surprisingly, she found the tale hilarious and still does!

Some time after, Jimmy told us how he had been watching the news with his girlfriend when a report about Hurricane Rita came on, and every time they mentioned it he could see his girlfriend giving him dirty looks out of the corner of his eye!

'Couldn't they have called it something else?' he asked, feeling sorry for himself.

Around the time that Rita was there, Dariusz, our Polish lodger, moved out. Fortunately, we managed to replace him the same day with a quiet but seemingly pleasant Portuguese girl named Dina. She had drunk in the pub on several occasions and had started working for us the previous Thursday.

She phoned and spoke to Banana, saying that she was in her friend's car and that they had been unable to gain access through the bus station. When they finally managed to get through, General went down and carried Dina's luggage up for her. Dina, meanwhile, had remained downstairs in a deep discussion with her friend, who had long, dark, curly hair and was very attractive.

We all went back inside from the balcony (nosey bunch!), apart from my nephew, Christian, who stayed outside. After about five minutes, Christian came charging into the room.

'They're fighting downstairs!'

'Who is?'

'Dina and her friend! She's pulling her hair and punching her!' he revealed excitedly.

We rushed out onto the balcony, to be greeted by screaming and shouting and the sight of the other girl standing there, bruised and battered.

'She went crazy and started punching and kicking me!' she explained to us, in between loud sobs.

Dina suddenly reappeared and glared at her 'friend' with a manic expression on her face.

'Dina, just think what sort of an impression you are giving your future landlords and employers!' she warned.

However, Dina was oblivious to our presence and marched

towards the girl as she got back into the car. She leant through the car window and began telling her off in lowered tones, before suddenly walking around the front of the car to the passenger side. She yanked the door open, climbed inside and then launched a further frenzied attack on the other girl. After a minute of this, Dina jumped out of the car, grabbed her luggage, which General had taken back downstairs, and put it in the boot. She got back in the car and off they went, never to be seen again (by us, anyway). Did we have a lucky escape? Or perhaps it would have livened things up upstairs, especially when Dina had her 'friend' or 'friends' staying over!

In the usual after-fight inquest, Banana exclaimed excitedly, 'She was probably planning to rape me!'

After she repeated it the third time, General responded, 'I'm sure that's your fantasy, Banana!'

'General, how could you say such a thing?' she replied in mock horror.

Terry the Busker

'Terry the Busker' was a big, broad, tough-looking Scotsman who used to march into the pub with his guitar in his hand to have a few pints with his Irish girlfriend, Mary, who was a traffic warden. They were sometimes a bit crazy, but were a nice couple, who all the regulars knew.

Terry was always getting into punch-ups on the Underground, where he would play his guitar to earn his 'beer money', resulting in his frequently coming in with a black eye or cut face. Mind you, I would have bet that the other bloke or blokes came off worse, as he was a hard man with an interesting past.

In the late seventies, he was at a party when the couple whose place it was began arguing. The woman had just started a fry-up for the guests when, during the course of the argument, her partner grabbed the frying pan and threw the contents all over her. The others all rushed into the kitchen when they heard her screams, and it did not take them long to realise what had happened. Some of them went immediately to the lady's aid, while Terry, understandably, launched an attack on the man, giving him a deserved good hiding. It was, of course, the end of the party, as the injured woman was taken to hospital while her partner was lying in a heap on the settee.

In the early hours of the following morning, Terry's door was kicked in and he was dragged out of bed by several police officers, who arrested him and took him to the police station. Terry would not see the outside world for another thirteen years, as the man he had given a beating to the previous night had since died, resulting in Terry, ludicrously, being charged with murder.

Terry ended up in Rampton Hospital, where Ian Brady is kept. He told us how that bastard Brady would be attacked by other inmates, but would, incredibly, return the next day and plonk himself on a seat right in the middle of the very same group that had attacked him. They would give him another hiding, only for Brady to do exactly the same the next day.

Terry was another one who we liked, and, if he ever got really drunk, we would let him crash out upstairs. He would have been as good as a guard dog if anyone had tried to break in!

My mate Sean celebrated the birth of his son, Kai, by coming down the Duke with some other mates, Darren, Jamesy, Dr Lake, Beefy, Paul B., Dean, Mark and Peter, to wet the baby's head. We had a good drink until about 2.30 a.m., when they left to get a cab home. However, they got something to eat and were back knocking on the door at 3.00 a.m., just as I was getting into bed. I went down and let them back in, and we started all over again. That was a typical Saturday night in the Cambridge.

There used to be a chubby, jovial bloke called Colin, who looked like Mr Bumble in *Oliver Twist*. He used to pop in every few days for the odd pint and sit at a table, yelling across to whoever was serving behind the bar.

'Where do you live, Colin?' I asked him.

'Hounslow.'

'Yeah, but where exactly?'

'A couple of doors away from Scouse Steve,' he replied.

Later on, I happened to mention it to General and we thought of a wind-up. Every time Colin came into the pub, we would say the same thing.

'Oh, Colin, by the way, Scouse Steve was talking about you.'

'Oh, yeah? What was he saying, then?'

'He said he'd like to see you and that you're welcome to pop round for a cup of tea any time you like.'

'That's very kind of him. I might take him up on that.'

A couple of days later, Steve came bursting into the pub.

'You bastards, sending that Colin round my place!' he shouted at us. 'I couldn't get rid of him!'

'We wouldn't do that, Steve,' General protested.

'I know it was you!' Steve responded.

The following day, Colin came in for his pint and revealed straight away, 'I went round Steve's for that cup of tea, but he seemed a bit shocked to see me.'

'No, he was just pleasantly surprised,' I assured him.

'Why, what did he say?' Colin enquired enthusiastically.

'He said that he really enjoyed your chat and that you're welcome round there whenever you feel like it,' I said convincingly.

'That's terrific; I'll do that!' he shouted, as pleased as punch.

When Steve came walking in that evening, we got Scottish Dave to call out, 'Oi, Steve, Colin said "get the kettle on"!'

'He's driving me mad! As soon as I get home, he's banging on my door, saying the same thing: "Just popping round for a cuppa, Steve." I blame you two, you bastards!' he would say to General and I, while we both stood there, looking innocent.

'The Brothers Grimm are at it again!' shouted Gurmit.

Scottish Dave had a bit of a love affair going with an old lady called Jeannie, who was a right character. She called every other bloke in the pub 'sir' apart from Dave, who she called 'Sweetie Pie', as she adored him. She would sit in the corner and shout out, while Dave was propping up the bar, 'How's my little Sweetie Pie?'

She even said that he could move in with her and that she would happily do all his laundry and cooking for him.

'And I'd even let my little Sweetie Pie in my bed once a week as well!' Jeannie added.

Dave seemed to be giving it some serious consideration, especially after a few pints.

'I've had worse offers!' he commented.

It struck us that Jeannie had had a sad life and used to come in to enjoy the company in the Cambridge. She used to travel from Surbiton, about ten miles away, and always seemed reluctant to leave for home.

'I won't live past Christmas,' she started telling everyone in October 2005, before changing it to 'I'll be dead by Boxing Day.'

She came in just before Christmas, when we gave her a Christmas card and a little present, and then we never saw her again, so, to this day, we do not know whether her prediction came true.

An Eventful Night

Bradley Lee was a legendary figure around Hounslow. He was well over twenty stone and had 'Made in England' tattooed across his forehead. He had been absolutely massive as a schoolboy as well. He was identical to Terry the leader of the Baldies in the film *The Wanderers* and could no doubt be quite intimidating to some people, although I always found him polite and pleasant.

However, there was always the feeling that, wherever he was, trouble would not be far behind. Moreover, there had been rumours that he had made a fourteen-year-old girl pregnant. I hoped that this was untrue, as there were always rumours of one sort or another being spread about by people in the pubs around Hounslow, which were a breeding ground for gossip. It always amazed me how quickly news or rumours were able to travel from pub to pub.

Anyway, one Saturday night, Bradley came into the pub with a couple of mates. They were having a quiet drink and were no problem. The peace was shattered however, when Sandra Dougan made her entrance. She was a local nutter, whose brother was a well-known name at Chelsea. What we did not know when Sandra walked in was that it was her daughter who Bradley had made pregnant. She was like a rabid dog when she saw him there, and she had to be pulled away.

'Chris, Davie Norton's outside!' Scottish John informed me.

'Shit, that's all I need!' He was one of the notorious Norton brothers, he was turning up tonight, of all nights, with Bradley Lee and Sandra Dougan already having to be kept apart.

'All right, Davie?' I said to him on the doorstep, where he was polishing off a kebab. He had a girl standing alongside him, who appeared to be quite pleasant.

'Can I come in or not?'

'No, you can't.'

'OK Chris; it's your pub,' he replied, to my surprise.

He walked along and looked through the side window, then noticed Bradley Lee drinking inside.

'Oh, I fuckin' get it! You won't let me in, but you let a fuckin' nonce in!' he protested.

'He's on about Bradley Lee,' explained Scottish John, who had joined me in the doorway.

'Yeah, I gathered that,' I replied.

Davie pulled out his mobile and was immediately shouting into it. 'Get yourselves down the Duke of Cambridge, because that nonce Bradley Lee's in there, drinking. Yeah, that's right, the Duke of fuckin' Cambridge!'

He was pacing up and down the road, shouting at the top of his voice.

'One thing I can't stand is fuckin' nonces!'

'I know you can't, Davie. Come on, let's just go,' the girl said calmly. She was a great help, unlike a lot of the girls around Hounslow, who seemed to thrive on stirring up trouble.

John stood guard at the door for me as I went back inside in search of Bradley Lee. As I mentioned previously, he had always been polite and courteous to me, so that was the only way I could judge him. However, if what the others were saying about him turned out to be true, then I would not want anything more to do with him.

Sandra was still extremely agitated and being egged on by two mouthy travellers, so the situation was deteriorating rapidly.

'Bradley, can I have a word?'

'Of course, Chris; what's the problem?'

'Davie Norton's outside…'

'That doesn't bother me!' he interrupted.

'Maybe not, but it bothers me, and I don't want our pub getting wrecked over it. Look, he's on his mobile, getting people down here, so, if you want, I can let you out the back way, so as to avoid them.'

'Thanks very much for the offer, Chris, but I came in the front way and I'll go out the front way, if you don't mind,' he insisted.

'OK, if that's what you want,' I agreed.

Harry and Malcolm had been joined by Scottish John in trying to pacify Sandra, who was becoming more and more aggressive. I let Bradley out with his two mates and watched them walking up the road towards Hounslow East Underground Station. I then noticed Bradley pulling a bottle out from inside his jacket. He did not appear to be unduly worried by any threat to him that night. I watched to see whether Davie Norton and his mates would make a show, but they were nowhere.

'Are you OK, Sandra?' I asked, after going back inside. 'He's gone now.'

'No, she ain't all right!' shouted one of the travellers.

'Sorry, was I talking to you?' I asked.

'Well, I'm tuckin'—' He did not finish what he was saying, as Malcolm grabbed him and dragged him through the crowd towards the porch.

'Oi, you tuckin' leave my brother—' The other one did not have a chance to finish his sentence, as Harry grabbed him by the scruff of the neck and dragged him into the porch.

'Chris, come and get this door unlocked!' shouted Scottish John, who had joined them in the porch.

I walked out and unlocked the door. As soon as I pulled it open, the two drunks were thrown out into the street. They approached the door again and looked at Harry, Malcolm and John before deciding against starting anything with any of them. I moved forward to close the door when one of the bastards took a free punch at me. I was livid, so returned the compliment by hitting him three times in the face with the keys in my hand, causing his face to be marked all over.

'He'll be able to go and get a set cut tomorrow!' Scottish John cracked when we were back inside.

Mistaken Identity

Malcolm covered all day Sunday for us for the last couple of years. This was a real plus, as he was honest and reliable and would not stand any nonsense from anyone.

One Sunday evening, I returned to the pub, only to be called aside by Malcolm.

'You might be getting a phone call later.'

'Who from?'

'There were a few Indian blokes in here earlier on, sitting at that table by the jukebox. I didn't notice anything really going on, but, about half an hour after they had left, there was a phone call and one of them claimed that they were abused in here. He then said that the bloke followed them outside as they were leaving and threatened them,' Malcolm explained.

'Did you see anything?' I asked him.

'No, nothing like that. I mean, Duncan was in here, with a Glasgow Rangers mate of his and Tim and a few others. They were a being a bit loud, but I didn't notice them even say anything to those Indian blokes.' Tim was a huge bloke, a postman who could sink a few pints.

'Oh, well, he probably won't even phone back,' I commented.

The following day, General was working behind the bar when he received a telephone call. He came upstairs and said to me, 'There's somebody on the phone called Dhiron. He's on about some incident in the pub yesterday and how he's going to contact the police if he doesn't get any satisfaction from us. Do you know anything about that?'

'Yeah, Malcolm said something about it yesterday. I'll speak to him,' I replied.

'Good afternoon. I hope that the barman has told you about the racist abuse I suffered in your pub yesterday afternoon,' he began in a businesslike tone.

'He mentioned something about it. What sort of racist abuse was it?' I enquired.

'He was calling us bastards and told us to fuck off several times.'

'How's that racial abuse, then? It sounds like straightforward abuse to me.'

'To be honest, it is treated more seriously if it is classed as racial abuse,' he pointed out.

'Maybe, but if it isn't then it isn't and, to be honest, I can't stand all this political correctness, so, if you want to go down that road, we'll end this conversation right now,' I scolded.

'I could always take it up with the authorities,' he threatened.

'Why should I treat this more seriously than if it had been a white person abusing another white person or a black person abusing a group of Asians?'

'Oh, no, I entirely agree with you,' he enthused. 'I cannot stand political correctness either.'

How strange, he had totally changed his tune in the space of two minutes.

'That's OK, then. So long as we understand each other. Go on, then; tell me what happened.'

'I am sorry for starting off in that way, but I am very upset because my dad was with us and he is getting on a bit, and it was the first time anything like this had ever happened in your pub. We have always felt extremely comfortable there,' he explained.

'Look, Dhiron, I can understand why you are upset. I was out with my family yesterday and, if somebody had abused my parents, I would have gone mad,' I said, in a much friendlier tone.

'OK, you obviously understand how I feel, then, if you are close to your family. Anyway, I came into the Duke of Cambridge with my dad and my brother. We were sitting at the table and there was a rowdy group at the bar. Suddenly, one of them approached our table and started annoying us.'

'Did the barman say anything?' I asked, knowing full well that Malcolm would in a situation like this.

'He came up to the table and said to just tell them to go away if any of them were bothering us, which we thought was a bizarre thing to say, as it was surely his job to do that.'

'That doesn't sound like Malcolm,' I retorted. 'He would have no qualms about telling anyone to behave.'

'The man continued glaring at us and making comments, so we decided to leave, but, as we were leaving, he followed us out of the pub and challenged us to a fight.'

'What happened next?' I asked, amazed, as I was sure that Malcolm would have noticed this going on. *Maybe, he was down the cellar*, I thought to myself.

'His friends came to the door and shouted for him to come away, and they pulled him back inside.'

'What did he look like? Was he a great big bloke?' I asked.

'No, he wasn't really big. He was only about average,' Dhiron recalled.

It wasn't Tim, then, I thought to myself, as Tim was huge.

'He was about average size, shortish hair.'

'Did he have a Scottish accent?'

'He could have done.'

It could have been Duncan, then, I thought to myself. He was a nice bloke, but he could sometimes get paranoid after a few drinks. *Mind you, the bit about following them outside doesn't sound like Duncan...*

My thoughts were interrupted as Dhiron continued. 'His name might have been Archie.'

'Archie? We haven't got anyone called Archie drinking in here.'

'Well, all the others drinking in there knew him, because they were shouting, "Come on, Archie, leave it!"'

I suddenly remembered that Duncan's mate had been drinking in the pub and decided that it must have been him, although I was not going to tell Dhiron. I would deal with it myself.

'I'll call my brother and ask him, but I am certain that his name was Archie,' he stressed.

About ten minutes later, General came upstairs to tell me, 'That was Dhiron again. He said to tell you that the man responsible was definitely called Archie.'

'It must have been Duncan's mate, then,' I concluded. 'Malcolm said that Duncan had a mate in, watching the Glasgow Rangers game.'

'No, his name's Alex,' General informed me. 'He's been here before with Duncan. Anyway, he said he's going to come in tonight at half seven to try and sort it out here before he takes it any further.'

'Shit, this is all we need.'

About an hour later, General came upstairs again.

'You won't believe this. He's been on the phone again.'

'What does he want now?' I asked impatiently.

'He started off by saying, "this is the most difficult phone call I have ever had to make, but I got the wrong Duke of Cambridge!"'

'You're joking!' I shouted in disbelief. 'What did he say next?'

'He said it wasn't the one in Hounslow, it was the one in Whitton, and he apologised.'

'Apologised! We could have barred somebody for nothing,' I protested.

'I know; he could have caused a load of trouble,' agreed General.

However, after a few seconds, we started laughing, as we had to see the funny side of it!

'You know who it is. It must be Swanny's mate, Archie!' announced General.

'Oh, yeah, of course, he drinks in there,' I agreed.

That was the amazing thing about it: we did know the culprit, after all!

Frankie

We had our own personal security man round the back of the pub. He was a night cleaner on the buses and looked like a cartoon character, as he was round, bald and always shouting and laughing like a lunatic. His name was Keith, but I originally wound Banana up telling her his name was 'Frankie'. From that day onwards, she always called him Frankie, and, incredibly, Keith never once corrected her, even when she introduced him as Frankie.

He would always greet us by saying, 'Hello, Chris; all right, my son?' or 'Hello, Preshan; all right, my darling?' For some strange reason, he thought her name was Preshan. That had nothing to do with me, as even I would not have been able to think up a name like that!

Whilst chatting one night, we discovered that he had grown up next door to our grandparents in Sunbury.

'How are Benny and Ivy?' he asked me, the next time I saw him.

'They died years ago,' I explained, surprised that he could have thought they were still alive, as he had lived next door to them in the sixties.

When I went upstairs, I told General what Frankie had just said.

'Well, he would just remember them like they were all those years ago, as he hasn't seen them since.'

A couple of weeks later, General pulled up in his car with his sons, Christian and Glenn, and his daughter, Shannon. Frankie charged over to the car.

'Hello, Charlie; all right, my son?' he greeted General, as I had told him months before that General's name was Charlie.

'Benny and Ivy were asking about you, Frankie,' General told him.

'Really? How are Benny and Ivy?' he asked, obviously totally forgetting what I had told him only two weeks before.

'They're fine! They told me that you were a bit of a hooligan in your younger days,' General replied, continuing to wind him up.

'No, I wasn't!' he disagreed. 'But they used to make loads of noise with all their parties!'

That comment made us smile, as it had seemed that, every time we visited them, they would have some sort of party, and they had even had a bar in the front room!

Laia was our live-in Spanish cleaner, who had replaced a girl with whom we had had a lot of problems. Banana had already explained why we had had to get rid of the previous girl, but Laia seemed different. She was quiet, polite and did not drink too much.

One night, I was lying in bed when I heard voices out the back. Laia would sometimes bring her friend Ana back with her, which was not a problem, but this was a man's voice.

'Shit! Banana, Laia's brought a bloke back with her!' I exclaimed.

'You're joking. Oh, no; I thought she was different.'

We had a rule against this, as we did not want blokes who we did not know from Adam wandering around the pub when we obviously had the day's takings there, as well as all the stock. I walked into the living room without turning any lights on. Laia and her male accomplice were at the back door, trying to unlock it, which was not always easy. I waited behind the door and, when they unlocked it, I jumped out like Superman. To be honest, I was probably more like Batman!

'What you up to?' I shouted.

They both jumped out of their skin, screaming like mad, which caused me to jump back in shock.

'Chris, my son! What on Earth were you doing, jumping out on us in the dark like that? You nearly gave me a heart attack!' Laia's breathless and stunned companion complained.

'I'm sorry, Frankie, I didn't know who it was,' I explained.

'I... I was just helping the poor girl to get in, as she could not unlock the door,' he continued, trying to get his breath back.

Laia's face was a picture! She could only understand a little English at that time and must have wondered what was going on.

We started laughing and, before long, the three of us were doubled up with hysterical laughter.

If you are reading this, Frankie, I am sorry about that, and thank you for all your help!

While reading this, Maria looked up and asked Banana, 'Has he ever found out why you call him Frankie?'

'No; he's never asked!' replied Banana.

'Hasn't he ever told you that his name isn't Frankie?'

'No, he hasn't!'

Dangerous Danny

By far the maddest bloke in the pub during my time was a nutter called Danny, who was a regular when we took over the pub in 2000. He was not particularly tall, but was really broad and had scars all over his face. He also had a manic look in his eyes, as he always seemed to be out of his head on something or other.

Not long after we took over, he turned up one mid-week afternoon with blood all over his shoes. He disappeared into the toilets and, as he, at the best of times, was not exactly the quietest of people, I could hear every word he was saying or, more precisely, screaming down his mobile.

'Look, all I wanna fuckin' know is if he's still alive,' he shouted furiously, followed by, 'Shit, that's all I fuckin' need!'

Listening to the rest of the conversation from his side, I concluded that he had given a bouncer at a West End club a severe beating and that the bouncer was on a life support machine.

On another occasion, he was propping up the public bar when Donegal Don came into the pub with Jeff, who was a brilliant pool player, although he could be really flash about it sometimes. They had a couple of games together before Jeff shouted out a challenge to Danny, who he obviously did not know.

'Oi, mate, want a game for a score?'

'Yeah, all right,' Danny replied.

They had a game, closely monitored by Dave, which Jeff, unsurprisingly, won.

'Double or quits?' Jeff asked Danny, after pocketing his winnings.

'OK,' Danny replied gruffly.

'Get yer money out, then,' commanded Jeff.

'You fuckin' what?' demanded Danny.

'If you wanna play double or quits, let me see your money,' insisted Jeff.

I was behind the bar and was waiting for the eruption, as I had witnessed Danny losing the plot on a couple of occasions.

'You wanna see my fuckin' money, you cheeky little shit! I just fuckin' paid you, didn't I?'

'Yeah I know but—'

'No fuckin' buts. I've a good mind to fuckin' sort out you out right now, you fuckin' cocky bastard!'

As Danny moved around the pool table to get nearer, Jeff would move in the opposite direction on the other side of the table. The penny had finally dropped that he was in big trouble. However, Danny must have realised he was not going to be able to get hold of Jeff like that.

'I'll tell you what. I'll play you for a fuckin' monkey! We'll see how fuckin' good you really are then. I'll be back in twenty minutes; make sure you've got the readies!' he yelled, before storming out of the door, slamming it behind him.

'You fuckin' idiot, Jeff! What you fuckin' doing, upsetting a nutter like him?' Dave scolded him.

'I ain't scared of him. I'll fuckin' bottle him if he comes back and starts anything,' Jeff responded, trying to recover his composure. I do not think he was kidding Dave, and he certainly was not fooling me, as he had been petrified.

'You don't want to start anything like that with a maniac like him. He'll just pull a gun out and shoot you. He's your full "Lock, Stock and Two Smokin' Barrels" sort of bloke. You don't fuck around with the likes of him,' Dave lectured him. 'Chris, tell him what he's like,' he called out to me.

'He's a raving lunatic!' I confirmed.

Jeff looked seriously worried when I told him that, but he appeared frightened stiff five minutes later when the door flew open and Danny charged in like a raging bull.

'Right, you fucker! I've got 500 quid 'ere; are you playing or not?' Danny shouted as he dropped his jacket on the floor. It landed with such an echoing thud that it almost went through the floor to the cellar below. £500 did not make a noise like that, and Jeff and Dave knew it.

'I haven't got £500,' replied Jeff.

'Right, give me my score back right now!' Danny screamed, almost frothing at the mouth.

Jeff rifled through his pocket for the score, while continuing to make sure that the width or breadth of the pool table was between him and the madman trying to get at him. He threw the twenty-pound note on the table, and Danny grabbed it and shoved it in his pocket in an instant. He then began chatting as if nothing untoward had occurred and the three of them were old friends.

On another occasion, when I was out, Danny started having a go at Michael, who was working behind the bar. Scouse Steve stepped in to calm the situation down.

'Oh, I get it: you're the heavy on the firm!' he said accusingly to Steve.

'No, I'm not! I'm just a partner in the business and I don't want any trouble in this pub.'

The conversation continued, and Steve asked Danny to leave the premises. They went outside the public bar, where Steve patiently tried to get him to go home quietly. Steve still had his pint with him and was supping it as he continued speaking to Danny.

'Look, Danny, go home now, as you've had a bit too much, and then you can come back tomorrow without any problems.'

'Are you sure? All right, then,' was Danny's response, much to Steve's relief.

'I'll see you later, then, Danny!' Steve called out, moving around him to go back into the pub.

'Oi, you fuckin' bastard!' Danny screamed at him.

'What's up now, Dan?' asked a bemused Steve.

'You were getting ready to glass me there!' was the accusation he levelled at Steve.

He had completely changed again. Steve managed to keep calm and eventually got rid of him. He came back into the pub, looking in desperate need of another pint.

'Where's Michael?' Steve asked Michelle, who was behind the bar.

'He's gone upstairs for a break,' explained Michelle.

'You're joking! I stuck my neck out there, helping him with that nutter, and I thought he'd at least be in here, watching my back.'

About a month later, it was approaching closing time and Danny was at the bar, beginning to be a bit of a pain. There was no way that I would let him stay for a late drink. It took me about fifteen minutes to get rid of him before I locked up and returned to Neilson, General and a couple of girls who had stayed for a drink. It was always difficult to get rid of people when it was obvious to them that others would be staying after hours.

I was just starting to relax and join in the banter when there was a really loud din of someone thumping on the window. I rushed out into the porch to be greeted by the sight of Danny standing on the doorstep, with blood running from his nose from a bit too much snorting.

'I've left twenty quid on the bar!' he yelled.

'Oh, yeah. Look, Danny, there's no money on the bar or anywhere else!' I shouted back at him.

'I'm fuckin' tellin' yer. I left twenty quid on that bar and I want it now!'

'I'll go and have a look for it,' I replied.

If I don't give it to the fuckin' nutter, at the very least he's gonna put the windows in, and it could be even worse, I thought to myself. I knew then that I would have to give it to him, and that made me a hypocrite, bearing in mind what I had said to Fitzy, although they were different circumstances. This lunatic was quite capable of burning the pub down during the night while everyone was in bed.

However, I made up my mind then that he had to go for good, and I did not have long to wait, as, the next day, I had just opened up and was putting the ashtrays on the tables when in he came, as bold as brass.

'Morning, Danny.'

'All right, Chris? A pint when you're ready.'

'No, sorry, Danny; I'm not serving you.'

He stopped dead in his tracks and, with eyes blazing, asked in his usual polite way, 'What do you mean, you ain't serving me? Why the fuck not?'

"Cause I've had some complaints about you. You're scaring the customers' (not to mention me!) 'so I've got no choice.'

'Right, I'll tell you something now...' he began.

Here we go, I thought, anticipating something nasty.

'You ain't the first guv'nor to say that to me and you won't be the last, but, because you've said it to my face like a man, I'm gonna shake yer 'and now and walk out of that door and never bother you again.'

'That's fine by me!' I replied, trying to hide my relief.

Danny shook my hand and walked out of the door, and that was the last I ever saw of him, as he was good to his word and never bothered us again.

Clearing Out

Clive was a regular before we took over and frequented the pub the first year we were there until I eventually barred him. He was a big, fair-haired bloke of well over six feet who had done time for manslaughter, but I felt that he was a bit of a bully and I knew others who thought the same. He was certainly scared of Danny and was delighted when he found out that he had been barred. Clive took a great deal up his nose and, in addition to the many pints of cider he would polish off, it would make him paranoid. One day, I had just walked into the corridor when I heard his voice coming from the toilet.

'No, Clive, don't be stupid. You don't want to do that; they're nice people in here!' he was shouting.

After he came out of the toilet, I walked in there and, sure enough, it was empty, so he had been talking to himself, unless, of course, he had been chatting on his mobile to some other bloke called Clive!

Eventually, I lost patience with him, as I had received complaints about him intimidating some of the regulars. Before we had taken over, he had beaten Richard and Duncan up on different occasions. One night, I followed him into the toilet, knowing full well that he would be snorting some Charlie in there.

'Right, come on, Clive; out you go!' I insisted, after catching him in the cubicle with the powder all spread out and ready.

'Let me just do this first,' he protested.

'No way; you're going now,' I insisted.

We went out the back entrance, where we stood talking for about half an hour.

'Go on, give me one more chance,' he pleaded.

'No, I've made up my mind now,' I stressed.

Suddenly, without any warning, he broke down in tears and began to sob uncontrollably. I stood and waited in silence for what seemed like ages for him to finish crying. I almost felt sorry for him as he leant on my car with his head in his hands.

'Is everything all right, Chris?' Harry asked, popping his head out of the back door. They must have been wondering where I had disappeared to.

'Yeah, fine, Harry.'

Clive eventually pulled himself together and went off home. He came in a month later, shouting out, 'Taxi! Has anyone ordered a cab in here?'

I went straight over to where he was standing.

'Come on, Clive, let's go. You know you're not allowed in here,'

'Have you seen my new motor outside?' he enquired. 'Come outside and have a look.'

I followed him out of the front door to where his car, which he was obviously very proud of, was parked. We chatted for about ten minutes, then we shook hands and he got in his car and drove away. He did not come in the pub again in my time there. It just goes to show that it does not always end in violence when you have to bar someone, even the nutters.

Clive's mate and drinking partner, Perry Ikes, was a different case, though. He was a big, stocky scaffolder with one eye, who had enjoyed quite a reputation around the Hounslow area. He used to come in with his wife, who would go berserk every now and again. On one occasion, she threw a chair at a bloke having a drink at the bar, so Gypsy Alan and I escorted her out, informing her she was barred. Meanwhile, Ikes stayed in the pub, propping up the bar, drinking.

'I'm sorry about her, Chris, but that was nothing to do with me. She's out of control sometimes,' he informed me.

'I can see that!' I agreed.

A lot of customers told me they were happy that she had been barred, not because of the trouble she would periodically cause but because she had the loudest laugh you could possibly imagine. It was more of a continuous shriek and would go right through you.

Ikes had had a go at me a couple of years previously. He had been in with the wife and the rest of the family one Sunday night, and I let them stay for a late one. About 12.30 a.m., they asked me to call a cab. When it turned up, they would not finish their drinks, so the cab driver drove off. After about fifteen minutes, they asked me to call another one.

'I'll call you one, but you'd better go as soon as he gets here,' I told them. I did not like messing the cab companies around, because then, when customers genuinely needed one, the cab firm could refuse to send one.

The cab pulled up outside and I had a real struggle getting them to drink up and leave, but finally managed it. Harry was still there, having a drink with his girlfriend Carla, and there were a couple of other people around. Suddenly, there was the sound of somebody thumping on the door, so I marched into the porch.

'What do you want, Perry?'

'Let me back in.'

'What?'

'Let me back in. I want another drink.'

'No, sorry; I'm closing now,' I told him.

'There's other people drinking in there. What's wrong with me?' he demanded to know.

'They're finishing up now, anyway,' I explained.

'Open this fuckin' door and tell me!' he suddenly shouted.

'Hold on, then; I'll go and get the keys.'

I got the keys, went back into the porch and unlocked the door. He made a move as if he were going to come back into the pub, but I held the door firmly and stood in his way.

'So you ain't gonna let me back in for one more?'

'No; I've told you already. I've finished tonight. The others are just finishing up, and then I'm going to bed.'

'So, you're happy taking my money all day and then you chuck me out,' he said.

'I didn't chuck you out; you left!' I reminded him. This was a familiar complaint by customers who were not getting their own way.

'Don't you give me any fuckin' lip or I'll lay you out!' he threatened.

'You what?' I asked.

'I said, if you give me any more mouth, I'm gonna lay you out!'

'I'll tell you what, Perry: you go ahead any time you want, but you might get a bit of a surprise!' I warned him, almost slamming the door in his face.

He apologised the next time he came into the pub and was not any problem for the next couple of years, until one afternoon, when I came down to give Carmel a hand behind the bar, as she was really busy. The first person I noticed as I walked into the bar was Ikes.

'Oi, you wanker, get me a drink!' he yelled at me.

'I'm sorry?' I asked him, although I had clearly heard what he had said.

'You fuckin' heard! Get me a drink!'

'Perry, do me a favour. Don't speak to me like that, or you won't be getting a drink in here again,' I said.

'What've you got the hump about?' he demanded to know.

'Well, to be honest, I don't really like being spoken to like that,' I snapped at him.

'Oh, I get it. You come down here in a bad mood and take it out on me!' he yelled across the bar.

'I wasn't in a bad mood. In fact, I was in quite a good mood until you started insulting me!' I replied, aware that everyone around the bar was watching and listening with interest to what was going on between us.

'I'll tell you what: you come round here and I'll knock you out!' he threatened.

'What?'

'You heard me. Come round here and I'll knock you out!' he reiterated.

I grabbed the set of keys from the hook, walked along the bar, lifted up the bar flap and walked along to where he was leaning on the bar.

'Go on, then. What are yer gonna do now?' Ikes asked.

'Nothing. You said you were gonna knock me out, so I'm waiting.'

'What are you holding those keys for? Gonna hit me with 'em, are yer?'

'Why would I want to do that?' I asked, although I had already made up my mind that, if he made a move, his good eye was the target for the keys. I knew I could not let him hit me first, as he must have been sixteen or seventeen stone of muscle, not fat.

'Come on, boys, calm it down,' advised Ricardo and a builder who was working on the Underground, as it was being renovated at the time. 'Go back round there and calm down.'

Choosing to follow the advice, I went back round the other side of the bar and started giving poor old Carmel a hand. I served a couple of people, but kept an eye on Ikes, who was chatting to Ricardo and the builder.

'Chris, can I have a drink?' Ikes asked me.

He had not apologised and had asked as if he just expected me to say yes, and this antagonised me. I felt in no mood to bury the hatchet (apart from in his head).

'No, you can't. I'm not serving you again,' I insisted.

'Come on, let's forget it,' he urged.

'Look, I don't care what you say, you ain't having another drink!'

'Come on, mate, he's apologised, so let him have a drink,' his new mate, Bob the Builder called out.

'He hasn't apologised, he ain't getting another drink and you can mind your own business!' I told him angrily.

At that moment, General came in the back way and walked behind the bar, carrying a box of stuff.

'Oi! You come round 'ere and I'll knock you out as well!' Ikes shouted at him.

'What have I done?' asked General in amusement, not bothered in the slightest.

However, that was the final straw for me, and I completely lost my temper with him. I picked up a bottle that was on the bar, looked him straight in the eyes and told him, 'Come on, then, you fuckin' bastard! If you want some, let's fuckin' go now and I'll smash this straight in your fuckin' face!'

The colour drained from his cheeks as he lost his nerve. His builder mate took him away as Ricardo calmed me down.

'Come on, Chris, put the bottle down. You're a landlord; you can't be seen to be threatening people with bottles.'

'I know, but that fuckin' bastard—'

'Look, Chris, I know what he's like and I would be fuming if he had behaved like that to me, but you can't react in that way. Not in here, anyway, with all these people watching.' Richard spoke to me in a typical Scottish authoritarian manner, but in a way that let me know he sympathised with me. It had the desired result, and I put the bottle back on the bar before approaching Ikes. He looked at me and held out a hand, inviting me to shake it.

'Stick your fuckin' handshake up your arse, you wanker!' I shouted. 'You ever fuckin' come in 'ere again and I'll be ready for you!' I warned him, shaking with anger. Fortunately, he never came in again, although people would often tell me how he had told them that he was going to sort me out.

Polish Punch-Ups

There was a bizarre incident one mid-week night in the pub. There were not many regulars in there, but, noticeably, there were two groups of who I thought were Poles. As it turned out, one of the groups was Lithuanian, not Polish, and, being neighbours there was no love lost between these two. Within a couple of hours, a confrontation had started between the two groups.

'Come on, cut it out now. If you want any trouble, go outside and fight!' I shouted out as I stood between the two groups.

'Yes, of course,' they replied politely, and, with that, all the blokes marched to the door and out into the street to have a punch-up, while the girls continued sitting at each table, chatting and drinking.

The fight went on for about five minutes, which is a long time for a fight. They were rolling around in the road at one stage, with buses and cars swerving to avoid them. The punch-up fizzled out; they all dusted themselves down and then all came back to the door, where I stood, blocking their entry.

'Sorry, boys, you can't come back in.'

'Why not?' one of them asked.

'Because you've been fighting!' I explained, trying to hide a smile.

'Yes, I know, but we did what you said and went outside to fight. And our jackets and our girlfriends are inside, and we just want to drink. The fight is over.' He sounded like Lech Wałęsa!

I could not really argue with that, as everything he had said was true, so I stood aside and let them back in. I watched them as they sat down at the same tables they had sat at before and continued drinking and chatting as if nothing had happened. The two groups did not say another word to each other or even look at each other for the remainder of the night. At closing time, both groups left without any further problems. It was like turning the clock back to the fifties or sixties, and I thought it was great!

On the whole, I found the Poles, Ukrainians and Lithuanians really good. The Poles sometimes liked a punch-up after a few drinks, but, then, so do the British. What you never saw were gangs of them attacking one person, mugging old women or molesting teenage girls, like some other ethnic groups in the area.

One Saturday night, General and I went out the back to fight two Poles and had a good punch-up with them with no carry-ons after. General gave me some stick over that, as he had been fighting the bigger one, who was about six-foot-four!

On another occasion, I was working behind the bar when two Polish blokes came up to the bar.

'Can you change this beer?' one of them asked, holding up a three-quarters-full pint of Guinness.

'Why, what's wrong with it?' I asked.

'That man just drank some of it by mistake,' he explained.

'Well, I'm sorry, but I can't change it for that reason.'

'You won't change it?' he shouted aggressively.

'No, I won't,' I replied.

He then picked up the glass and poured the contents all over the bar, bar stools and floor.

'There you are!' he announced, with great satisfaction.

I walked around the bar and straight up to him. His mate appeared to be having a go at him, but, as my knowledge of Polish was absolutely zero, I did not have a clue what he was saying to him.

'Come on, let's go!' I insisted, putting my hand on his arm to guide him to the door, although he was refusing to budge. He turned around in an aggressive manner, so I hit him in the face. We fought until it was broken up by some of the others and Scottish John ejected the Pole. He had ripped my shirt to shreds, which cheesed me off a bit, but apart from that I was unmarked.

About a month later, I was collecting glasses from the tables when I realised that a couple sitting at a table in the corner were this Polish man and his girlfriend. He muttered something to her as I looked over at him.

'Hello; how are you tonight?' he asked in a friendly tone as his girlfriend sat there, smiling.

'I'm fine, thanks. How are you?'

'I'm good, thank you,' he replied cheerfully, holding out an outstretched hand, which I shook before taking the empties up to the bar. The couple came in quite frequently after that, and they would always smile and be friendly. It was another example of how Poles do not hold a grudge after a fair fight.

More Regulars

By far the strongest bloke in the pub was Big Mark, a huge bloke who worked at Fullers Brewery and had no problems throwing around the full kegs of beer. We had a competition one day to see who could lift up a bar stool with one hand and keep it steady, which Mark won easily. As a man who loved a bet, he should have had a flutter on himself! However, what was a bit more of a shock was when I was sitting on one of the stools and Mark picked it up with one hand. He lifted it right up in the air and, although I would have been helpless if anything happened, I had total trust in him. He held it steady for a good seven or eight seconds – not bad, considering I must have weighed about eleven and a half stone – before placing the stool steadily back down on the floor.

Big Jack, the Tom Jones lookalike and one of the three Singhs, was best mates with an Irish labourer called Sean. Sean was a really strong, big drinking bloke with hands the size of shovels, but was nevertheless a real gentleman. Sean, Jack and Pete were really good mates who used to prop up the public bar together, drinking and chatting away. They always entered the quiz as 'the Three Amigos' and invariably did very well.

Sean had not been in for a couple of weeks, which was unlike him, and then Pete came in and broke the tragic news that Sean's body had been found in the River Thames. He had committed suicide. Everyone was really upset, particularly Pete and Jack. I went with them to Sean's funeral, and we went back to the pub and had some food and drinks in his memory. Sean's sister came over from Waterford and was really chuffed, as she had not realised that he had good friends and did not spend his time alone in his room. After he died, Pete could not bring himself to drink in the Duke any more and Jack changed bars, as he could not bear to drink in the public bar without Sean.

Another big bloke who frequented the pub was an Irishman called Kieran, who was well known in the area. He was a friendly, lively character who had a presence about him, and, although he was always polite, I do not think many people would have crossed him. He had a very harsh, gruff voice and was almost impossible to understand after he had had a few drinks.

One particular Friday night, he had had a skinful and was having a drink and chat with our barmaid, Carmel, and her close friends, Pat, Tracey and Annie. Pat is another big bloke, who became really popular in the pub, as you could always have a laugh with him. They were having a conversation about Ireland and their family backgrounds. Pat's family came from somewhere in the north of Ireland, and Kieran had heard of the family name, McCreesh.

'McCreesh! McCreesh! I know that name!' Kieran was shouting in a loud, strict voice. 'McCreesh, where... McCreesh why... Do you want a drink, McCreesh?'

'Kieran, do you mind? The name's Pat,' Pat pointed out in his polite manner.

'OK, McCreesh, no problem!'

'Kieran, please, my name's Pat. Call me Pat!'

'OK, Pat McCreesh.'

'Just Pat, Kieran. Pat's enough.'

'OK, Pat,' Kieran said, finally.

'At last, Kieran!' Pat said, delighted that he appeared to have finally got through to Kieran.

Kieran marched up to the bar to get a drink.

'McCreesh! McCreesh! Oi, McCreesh, what are you drinking?' Kieran shouted out at the top of his voice, as we all fell about laughing. Pat was fuming, but had to laugh in the end. Carmel, Tracey and Annie were sitting next to Pat the whole time, fighting to stop themselves from bursting out laughing.

After that night, whenever Pat walked into the pub, we would all start shouting, 'McCreesh! McCreesh! McCreesh!', eventually becoming 'McCreesh! McCreesh! McCreesh! We've got to get rid of McCreesh!'

Banana was always the most enthusiastic in chanting this. However, she did not show anywhere near as much enthusiasm when Gurmit would begin counting out loud in Italian, '*Uno, due, tre, quattro...*' before the rest of us would join in, chanting, 'Ciao,

Banana; ciao, Banana; ciao, ciao, ciao!' about ten times running.

There were two other regulars, called Grant and Aaron, who frequented the Cambridge for the first couple of years before eventually getting themselves barred. They were friends at the time, although they eventually had a serious fall-out, which, I believe, they have not patched up since.

Grant lived above one of the shops opposite the pub and had an unhealthy interest in young teenage girls, which was the reason he was barred from the pub, although there were many other reasons for which we could have barred him, including using the pub as his base to deal in drugs. He even bought a bunny rabbit to entice young girls to his flat. He was unemployed, registered as mentally ill and, because of this he had a two-bedroom flat with everything paid for. He also used to receive free medication, which he would then sell on to further line his pockets. Grant was also a very fast runner, as we witnessed when somebody from the pub crossed the road to bid him 'good night'.

You can gather from his CV that Grant was not the most popular person in the area, and that is an understatement. However, Aaron was, on the whole, quite popular. He was well-spoken and well-educated, which was rather surprising, considering he grew up in the area and went to the same school as me. The explanation behind this was that he spent his early years in either Singapore or Malaysia (I cannot be sure which one) and attended an international school there. How he ended up at a rough comprehensive school like Syon, God only knows.

Aaron was a real eccentric who loved singing and performing on stage and could brilliantly impersonate Frank Sinatra. Although we liked him, his behaviour became increasingly erratic. He was a real Jekyll and Hyde, and we were never sure which of these he was going to be each time he came in. He made Ricardo appear a picture of stability!

Aaron appeared to love himself and was extremely vain, but I always felt that, deep down, he was very insecure. His ex-girlfriend was a lovely girl called Nichola, and, shortly after they split up, Aaron announced his engagement to someone else. Nobody else had met this wonderful Brazilian girl of whom he talked non-stop for two weeks, leading up to the engagement. It was a warm afternoon on the day of his engagement, and Aaron was dressed smartly in a dark suit and white shirt. Everyone sat out the back, as it was such a lovely day, but Aaron's girlfriend was not there yet.

'She'll be here at 4 p.m.,' Aaron repeatedly responded to enquiries about her whereabouts.

The dark-haired Latina beauty turned up at four on the dot, and Aaron immediately got up and kissed her on the cheek before leading her by the hand to introduce her to everyone.

'This is my fiancée, Maria!' he announced to each person individually, with real pride in his voice.

However, there was something not quite right about the situation. Aaron had only kissed her on the cheek, and the girl did not appear to be too comfortable holding hands with him.

'Maybe it's shyness,' one of the regulars, who had also noticed, commented.

I was not in agreement with this, as the girl was anything but shy. In fact, she was oozing with confidence but just did not appear to be the happy, contented bride-to-be.

At 5.30 p.m., she got up to go. Aaron held her hand as they left the pub, but he was back ten minutes later, having walked her to Hounslow East Underground Station on the Piccadilly Line, five minutes walk from the pub. He made up an excuse as to why she had to go so quickly.

Everyone continued chatting and having a few drinks, while Aaron basked in being the centre of attention. Suddenly, everything fell deathly silent as Nichola came bursting out of the back. She walked straight up to Aaron.

'You absolute bastard! How could you do this to me after all I've done for you?' she screamed at him, throwing her full glass of wine straight in his face. It dripped all down his face onto his brand new suit. However, I had the feeling that Aaron was enjoying this and had somehow set it all up.

Meanwhile, Nichola was in floods of tears and I felt really sorry for her, but I had to make her leave. I felt really guilty at the door when she turned around and said to me, 'But, Chris, you don't know the full story. You don't know how much I've helped him, and then he treats me like this.'

We never saw Aaron's fiancée again, and, rather strangely, nobody ever mentioned her after that day.

'Ivor, what's the cost of an escort for half an hour?' Coventry Tony shouted out later that night.

Another unique character was a tall, skinny window cleaner called Henry. He was softly spoken, with a bit of a manic look in his eyes, and always reminded me of Norman Bates from the *Psycho* films. He was always coming in with a black eye or cuts and bruises all over his face when he had been beaten up in the kebab shop or on the way home. Initially, we all used to comment how it was 'out of order' to hit someone like Henry, who 'would not say boo to a goose'. However, we soon found out that this was not true, as, after a few drinks, he would become an argumentative and obnoxious bloke. He nearly got a hiding from Big Mark once, after giving him a load of lip, but, fortunately, Roland managed to restrain him.

On another occasion, he started on Scottish John about Scotland. He would ask anyone who was not from London, 'What are you doing down here? Why don't you go back up there?' or to wherever they were from. I had heard him say it to many people, including Tiziana, who was always able to shut him up when he started. He could not provoke John, however much he tried.

'Why did you have to come down here?'

'Why can't I come down here?' John asked him.

'Because this is England and you're from Scotland,' Henry retorted.

'But didn't I fight in the British Army, not the Scottish Army?' John asked, enjoying himself.

'But you always wanted to be separate,' Henry said.

'What do you mean "separate"?'

'Well, you put that fence there.'

'What fence? Where?' asked a puzzled John.

'That fence between England and Scotland,' explained Henry.

'Oh, that fence!' exclaimed John. 'That fence happens to be called Hadrian's Wall. Didn't you know it's a wall and not a fence?'

'Fence, wall; what's the difference?' asked Henry.

'You tell me, Henry. What's the difference between a wall and a fence?'

'Why do you always answer my questions with a question?' Henry asked, becoming increasingly irate.

'Who told you that?' John asked, as sharp as a needle.

On another occasion, General was telling an unruly group to leave when one of them went for him with a glass from behind. There was a bloke in the pub whom I shall also call John, and he saw what was happening, charged over and rammed the yob in the face with the thick end of the cue, knocking him out instantly. The bloke was out for the count, but, amazingly, made a sufficient recovery later on to glass a bouncer at a pub near to us, so John really did save the day for us.

Making Friends

During the day, a group of us would play Scrabble at the bar. Any four from Ivor, Tony Baloney, Scouse John, Harry, Raymondo, Livi, Rob, Richard, General and I would play. We had to bar Ged from playing, because he would argue over everything and pretend that he did not know the rules. He would also take so long to take his go, that we would all lose interest. We would often play three games, taking us up to early evening, when the others would start coming in. In our last year, we started playing poker and Texas Hold 'em and would sometimes have up to twenty people joining in, although we would have two tables of ten.

There were certain nights in the pub when anything up to twenty or so regulars would be congregated along and around the bar, all joining in the banter. These were often the best times and everyone would be joining in giving and taking stick, as Richard always had to if there were any delays on the Underground. It did not matter whether he was working or not; he would always be blamed for it. Ken and Dennis would be in there, having a few beers and joining in. Dennis was a dustman and used to come in wearing his bright green uniform. He was always loud; a typical chirpy Cockney sort of character. His language was appalling, though, with every other word a swear word. Only Swanny or Neilson were able to give him a run for his money on that, and on one occasion Banana had the three of them propping up the bar. I swear not just the air but the whole pub turned blue!

Before Ken got married, Dennis had been his lodger, and we all joked about how it must have been like *Men Behaving Badly* in that house. When they opened the fridge, it would no doubt have been full of cans of beer, with the odd bit of out-of-date cheese hidden at the back!

Norma would come in and join them, and Maria, who lived upstairs, would come down and join Malcolm, Gurmit, Ralph and the others for an after-work drink, although Malcolm and Gurmit often liked to sit on their own for a while in order to unwind. Resham, a bus driver, would come in every night and join in the banter in between putting all his money in the fruit machine. Duncan, Ged, Scouse John and Ruth would join Richard, and then, somewhere nearby, you would often find Livi, Habba and Ivor. Steve and Harry would come in on their way home and join Gurmit and Malcolm for a drink. Malcolm's friend, Teri, would come in with a group of girls, including, Louise, Clare, Katie and Jo. They were always a good laugh and had been coming in from when we first took over. Sometimes, Gurmit's cousin, Sanj, another gentleman, would join them. Martin – the old barman Ted's son, not the Martin suspected of sending the love letter – would sit on his stool at the end of the bar. Pauline and Scottish James would also come in and mix with everyone. They were a really nice couple, but the only problem was that none of us could understand what James was saying! He was from the Highlands, and even some of the other Scots, like Richard, Duncan and Jimmy, used to have difficulty understanding him.

Despite being in their own groups, they would all be calling out comments to each other and exchanging banter. There were frequent political debates, in which Scottish Dave was guaranteed to make an invaluable contribution.

'Shoot Tony Blair!' he would shout out every thirty seconds. That was his answer to all the world's problems! Mind you, there were quite a few others who agreed with him. Dave reminded me of Ives out of *The Great Escape*.

We had bus drivers, Underground workers, van drivers, security men, builders, painters and decorators, and many other different workers frequenting the pub. We also had 'Chris the Pilot' who was actually a BA captain; Tony Baloney who was a chartered accountant; Father Peter, a Jesuit; Kirpal, a History teacher, and Gordon, a retired Army Officer, so there was a real mixture of people and professions.

In addition to this, there were many others who used to come in regularly to have a pint or two on their way home from work. They might not have known the other regulars apart from by sight, but they would gradually begin to join in the conversations. People like Dick with his cider; or Richard, having his rum and Coke; Rav and Josh, in for their couple of Kronenbourgs, and Carlos the Spaniard, would come in for his couple of pints of lager and a game of pool. There was Charles, an Irishman, who would pop in for two or three pints of Guinness on his way home from work. He was a complete gentleman and had, in fact, run a pub many years before, so he was one of the few who understood what it was really like to run a pub. Maltese Tony would come in and ask for 'a pint of Georgie', which was, of course, a pint of Courage Best.

It is difficult to describe the togetherness and camaraderie shared by the regulars in the pub. Lifelong friendships were made in that pub, and it was a place in which somebody could come on their own and, so long as they were sociable, would be accepted into the fold. Then, within two or three weeks, they would not only know about thirty people by name, they would also know what they did for a living, where they lived and, more importantly, what each person drank. A lot of these people would have had a massive void in their life if they did not have the Cambridge, or pubs like ours, to go to. When locals like ours have disappeared, which will be pretty soon, and only the chain pubs are left, it will be a very sad day for many people all over the country. It just will not be the same when people will not be able to sit at the bar and have a drink.

The community spirit would not just be confined to the pub; it also existed outside. If anyone appeared to be in any trouble, you could guarantee that we would go and assist them. On one occasion after hours, General and I were upstairs when we heard a commotion outside. We looked out to see one man, aged about thirty, being abused and threatened by a mob of ten or twelve youths aged about eighteen or nineteen. We raced downstairs and called Harry, Scottish John and Raymondo before running down the road and chasing the youths off. The look of shock on their faces was great, as they must have wondered where we had come from. Fortunately, although the man, who was South African, had received a bit of a beating, he did not appear too badly hurt.

On another occasion, I was there on my own when I heard a

car driving up and down, braking and then revving the engine continuously. I looked out of the window and saw an Indian girl in a short, red dress staggering along the road. She was totally out of it and was heading to where the car making all the noise was now parked. It was full of young people of North African appearance, who began shouting out of the car at her, and then, suddenly, she lost her footing and landed on the pavement. I unlocked the door and rushed over to her.

'Are you OK?' I asked, noticing that she had cut and grazed her knees.

'Yes, I'm OK. I just want to get home,' she slurred.

'Look, I'll make sure you get home OK. There's a carload of blokes watching you; just tell them that you are with me if they say anything.'

She appeared to trust me, which was a pretty good choice at that moment, as the alternative did not look too good for her.

'Where do you live?'

She put her arms around my shoulder and I helped her along the road, past the youths in the car who stared but did not say anything more. I helped her up Cecil Road, which was the road opposite the pub, and round the corner to where she lived.

'They're bastards... doing this to me!' she repeated a couple of times.

'Who?' I enquired.

She said a couple of names which I cannot recall, but would not or was unable to explain what they had done, although I suspected they had tampered with her drinks.

'This is... I l-live there. The... brown door.'

I helped her right to the door and asked her if anyone was in.

'My boyfriend is in, but we mustn't wake him. I... I've got a key in... in my bag. Let me sit down for a second.'

Her legs gave way as she tried to sit on her doorstep and she dropped her bag, spilling the contents everywhere, and letting out a squeal as she slumped completely on the ground. I tried to help her sit up and then started to gather the items that had fallen out of her handbag. I had noticed the neighbours' lights go on and suddenly felt really uncomfortable. Just as I was thinking that I had to hurry up and get away, a police car pulled up and two officers jumped out of it.

'Right, what's going on here?' they asked.

I could be in trouble here, I thought to myself.

I explained that I ran the Duke of Cambridge and what had happened. They looked at the girl, who was muttering away. She looked in a terrible state, with her legs bleeding and her clothes dishevelled and half of her belongings still scattered all over the garden path.

'Is this true? Did this man help you to get home?' one of the officers asked her.

'Yes... he's been really nice.'

I was really relieved, as it had suddenly occurred to me that, if the girl had given a different answer, I could have found myself in a really sticky situation.

On another occasion, there was an elderly man standing outside in his dressing gown and pyjamas. He was peering through the window and then continuously looking in his wallet. I went outside and realised that he was extremely distressed. I called the girl I had been talking to outside as well, as I felt that this would make him feel more comfortable. He told us that he had left the hospital premises and got a bus, but some youths had taken his wallet from him and stolen all the money from it. We persuaded him to come into the pub, where we gave him a glass of water before I gave him a lift back to the hospital, where I discovered the staff searching frantically for him.

It was early evening when one of the regulars came into the pub and called out to me, 'Old Ted's collapsed out in the street.'

I went out to see if he was OK and quickly realised that he was paralytic drunk, so I went and got the car to give him a lift home. This was taking into consideration the fact that he had got drunk somewhere else, so he was not my responsibility, but, as he was an old man in his eighties, I had to help him. We pulled up outside his house and I helped him indoors, but, as I did, his wife, who was even smaller, started attacking him.

'I've warned you about coming home in this state!' she screamed at him. 'And you should know better, serving a drunken old man!' she yelled at me.

I protested my innocence, but it fell on deaf ears.

One night, West Ham Roland took Malcolm, Kirpal and I up

to central London, to his friend's pub. There was another Roland who drank in the pub: a black taxi driver who has been my mate for twenty-five years. To avoid confusion, we decided we would call him 'Roly Poly', although Federico had, naturally, called him Rolando.

Whenever Roly Poly came to the pub, we would sit up until the early hours, drinking and chatting about old times. When he finally got home, he would always give his wife the same excuse: 'Chris wouldn't let me out!' Karen, if you are reading this, the truth is that I could never get rid of him!

The pub West Ham Roland took us to was owned by the son of a famous person from the London underworld. He was a complete gentleman, but we all agreed that we would not have wanted to upset him.

'How long have you had your pub, then, Chris?'

'About three years.'

'Do you have any trouble?'

'Yeah, some, but not as much as we had at first,' I explained.

'We've had the odd bit lately with the Irish Travellers, haven't we?' Malcolm said.

'Yeah, we have,' I agreed.

'Well, I'll tell you what, if you get anything you can't handle, give me a shout, and we'll make a few enquiries and find out which group they're from and make sure they leave you alone,' he promised, with complete sincerity. It would have been that easy for them, which was an eye-opener to the power and influence this sort of people enjoy.

The Laughing Gnome

There was a little Welshman, called Kelvin, who used to come in every evening after work and down about six or seven pints of Kronenbourg. He was about five feet tall and had long hair and a beard. He was very rarely without his bobble hat and looked like a leprechaun. His only topics of conversation were rugby, his job over at the airport and, most importantly, the property he claimed he had bought in Spain. He was so obsessed that he was constantly bringing in brochures and maps of the area to show to anyone who could be bothered to listen. He then started insisting that he was Spanish and, if there happened to be any Spanish in the pub, then God help them, because Kelvin would make a beeline for them and then bore them for hours with his brochures.

'I'm not fuckin' Welsh; I'm Spanish!' he would yell out, night after night.

Then, one night, he came out with the classic comment. 'The next bloke who says I'm Welsh... I'm gonna knock his block off!'

Kelvin soon teamed up with Scottish Dave, another little Celt, who also used to also wear a bobble hat. We often wondered where their five mates had disappeared to! After a while, Dave, who had lived in the south of Spain, started shouting out 'I'm Spanish as well!' in support of Kelvin.

When Kelvin was getting drunk, he would shout out, 'I've got work in the morning, not like you bastards!', even though we all had to work the next day as well.

The last New Year's Eve we were in the pub, we had a live band called Food, who, that night, put on an even better gig than their usual high standard. They played for about four hours and did a great live version of 'Auld Lang Syne'. Kelvin was their number-one fan that night and started dancing and shouting in front of them when they were setting up the equipment at the start of the evening! He started shouting 'You English bastards can't sing or dance!', but nobody took offence, as everyone thought he was a character.

About 1 a.m., a girl came up to the bar in a bit of a panic and shouted above the music to General, who was working behind the bar.

'There's a man over there who urgently needs a cab, as he's really out of it!'

'Where is he, then?' asked General.

'That's him there. Look, he can't even stand up!'

'Oh, that's Kelvin. He's always like that,' General explained. 'He'll be all right.'

Just as General finished speaking, Kelvin lost his balance and spilt his drink over a crowd of revellers sitting at the table next to him.

'Chris, Kelvin needs to go; he's out of it,' General told me.

'OK, pass the keys and I'll let him out.'

I had to help Kelvin to the door, as he was incapable of walking on his own. He was not normally like this.

'Will you be OK, Kelvin?' I asked him, as he tried to find his balance while leaning on the wall outside.

'Yeah, I'll be all right,'

'Are you sure, Kelvin? Because I'm letting go now,' I warned him.

He just about managed to keep his balance as I let go. I then watched as he started to stagger down the road, before turning and rushing back inside, as it was a really busy night.

About ten minutes later, I went to let somebody out and, as I unlocked the door, I noticed that somebody was lying motionless in the middle of the road. I thought I had better go and help whoever it was get up. Besides the danger from the cars and buses that were swerving around him, the centre of Hounslow is not the safest place for a drunk to be having a New Year's siesta. As I got nearer, I realised that it was Kelvin lying there! I managed to get him up with the aid of a passer-by and decided that I would have to take him back into the pub and stick him upstairs for the night, as it was not safe for him to be lying around in the streets in the state he was in.

Tiziana fell in love with 'Auld Lang Syne' the first time she heard it and sang it with everyone in the pub, linking arms. The next day, she was telling everyone how much she had enjoyed it.

'It was a great night, and especially the song and dance we did at midnight!' she enthused.

'Auld Lang Syne.' I told her.

'Yes, "Old Lanes Lines"! I really love it! I want everyone to do it on my birthday night!' she insisted.

'You can't, Banana! It's a song especially for New Year's Eve,' Finnigan explained.

'Well, I want to do it for my birthday!'

On Banana's birthday night, she gathered everyone in a circle to do 'Old Lanes Lines', despite their protests. We all enjoyed doing it, really, even though it felt strange on 3 January.

'That was great! Let's do it again!' Banana shouted out, as everyone rushed away. 'OK, then. If we don't do it again now, we have to do it once a week!'

'For how long?' asked General.

'Until next New Year's Eve!' announced Banana.

That was not the only song title Banana got wrong. Another one was 'Chirpy Chirpy Cheep Cheep' by Middle of the Road, which Banana always called 'Chippy Chippy Chop Chop'! Nobody corrected her, and, in fact, we would all sing 'Chippy Chippy Chop Chop' whenever it came to the chorus! She also thought that 'Hit Me With Your Rhythm Stick' by Ian Dury and the Blockheads was actually, 'Hit Me With Your Wooden Stick', although I suspect Mr Neilson had something to do with that!

Banana and I went on a Health and Safety Course near the Old Bailey. At the end of the morning session, the instructor informed us that we would be sitting an exam at the end of the afternoon. Banana was horrified and started protesting.

'I won't be able to do it, because I'm not English and I won't be able to understand all the technical language they will use.'

'Well, why don't you try and see how you get on?' the tutor replied.

'No, I can't!'

'Look, just give it a try and you never know,' he continued.

Eventually, Banana reluctantly agreed to sit the exam and sat there, expecting the worst, when the results were read out.

'Four of you did extremely well by scoring twenty-nine out of thirty. Well done to you four!'

He read our names out before adding, 'But somebody here managed to get the perfect score of thirty out of thirty correct answers, and that was… Tiziana!'

Banana jumped out of her seat as if she had scored the winning goal in the World Cup Final, while everyone in the class cheered! The problem for me was that, whenever I tried making suggestions in the pub concerning health and safety, she would reply by saying, 'Look, I should have the final say, as I got a higher mark than you in the exam!'

Her next little trick was to put silver tinsel all around my certificate, with a sign saying 'Just passed!', and gold tinsel all around hers, with a sign saying 'Top of the Class!'

Harry and Malcolm's fortieth birthdays fell on the same day, so they held a joint party at the pub. I was playing the music and knew that Harry would be waiting for me to play a special request for him; his favourite record of all time: 'Mississippi', by Pussycat.

'This is a dedication to Harry. I know it's his favourite record and, as it's his special day, I would like everyone to sing along with him!'

Harry was up on the dance floor like a shot before he realised that 'his record' was the very apt 'Long-haired Lover from Liverpool' by Little Jimmy Osmond instead! I thought Harry would throttle me, but, after getting over the shock, he did his Eddie Yates laugh and then danced with one of his sisters!

Ralph and Arsenal Alan had an ongoing battle with Malcolm, Neilson and General on the music nights. Malcolm would request 'Blue is the Colour' and, as soon as Ralph heard that, he would charge up and request 'The Red Baron'. After Chelsea won the league, Malcolm would request 'We Are the Champions', which would provoke Ralph into asking for 'Shooting for the Gunners', but I had to draw the line at that.

This went on every Saturday night for two or three years, and then, during our last Christmas at the pub, Ralph and Alan presented Malcolm with a model of the Red Baron, which Malcolm still has on his mantelpiece.

A band called the Torpedo Pilots used to perform regularly in the pub and also used to drink in there quite regularly as well. They performed their own material almost exclusively and were very good.

Mike, the drummer, decided to have his Stag Night in the pub. He, like Frode, the lead singer, was Norwegian. Rather surprisingly, there were more women on the stag night than men, not that any of the regulars were complaining. Mike's dad was petrified of flying, so, he had not visited Mike during the eight or so years he had been living in England. He was marrying an American girl out in California, so he did not think he would be seeing his dad for any part of it. However, Frode and Chris, the other band members, had arranged for his dad to come over as a surprise for Mike. They set up all the gear on stage and did a rehearsal with Mike's dad on drums, and then, as Mike walked into the pub, they began playing a great version of Chuck Berry's 'Never Can Tell'. Mike always wore glasses, so it took him a while to realise that it was his dad playing the drums, but, after he realised, it was obvious to everyone how thrilled he was.

'I'm Your Radio' and 'We're Divine' were two of their records which went down particularly well with our regulars. I thought they were so good that I arranged for somebody high up in the music business to come and see them one Friday night. Unfortunately, Frode had an infection in his leg, so they had to cancel the gig. The problem for me was that the manager coming down from the music business was somebody with a big reputation in the London underworld, and I could not get through to him. I was trying all day, but all I could get was a fax machine, and I could not get in touch with his friend who ran a couple of local bars. I was panicking, but finally got through to him about 5.30 p.m., just before he was due to leave.

I explained what had happened and apologised to him, and I was pleased and relieved to hear his response.

'Well, thank you, son, for letting me know and saving me a wasted journey, and I'll tell you what: let me know next time they're playing, and I'll definitely come down and see 'em.'

Another group that performed in the Duke of Cambridge was the Insects, with my old mate Dapo on vocals. They always went down well and, like the Pilots, would always stay behind after the gig to have a few drinks and to mix with everyone. They are a band who, I think, will do well, especially with 'Country Boy'.

We had some other great bands, especially Food, who also went down well with all the regulars, with the exception of Malcolm and Ged, as they came down expecting something to eat!

No Going Back

One of the things we were really strict on in the pub was good manners. It might sound far-fetched, but for us it was really important.

In the early days of the pub, two Somalians came into the public bar, walked up to the counter and said, 'Two Stellas.' It was not in a particularly friendly tone of voice, either.

'I'm sorry?'

This was a tactic that usually worked, resulting in the person saying 'please' when having to repeat the order.

'Two Stellas!' one of them repeated, louder and more aggressively.

'You've got one more chance to ask properly,' I responded.

'What do you mean? What is up with you?' the man ordering the drink demanded to know.

'I'll tell you what's up with me. If you can't even say "please" in here when asking for a drink, then you're not getting served. You can go and get a drink somewhere else. I don't need your five pounds that badly.'

They stood there in shock before swearing and storming out of the pub.

A bus driver who was drinking in there at the time tried to excuse their behaviour. 'What you have to understand is that, in Somalia, to say "please" is seen as a form of begging,' he explained.

'Maybe that's so, but they're not in Somalia, they are in England, and, if they want a drink in this pub, they are going to have to say "please".'

On another occasion, Mo, a businessman who had taken over a coffee bar around the corner, came in with some of his workmen and friends. However, one of them was a young, flash Asian with an attitude.

'Stella,' he mumbled.

'Sorry?'

'Stella!' he repeated.

'We don't sell Stella,' I replied, in as an unfriendly tone as he had used.

'Kronenbourg, then.'

'Kronenbourg, what?' I asked.

'Pint of Kronenbourg!' he said in a louder tone, looking at me as if I were stupid.

'You've got one more chance to ask properly, or I'm not serving you,' I explained, beginning to lose patience.

'I asked properly!' he said, in a surprised voice. I looked at him and realised that he really had no idea, as that was the way he had always spoken and, almost certainly, nobody had ever pulled him up about it.

'The correct way to ask is to say, "A pint of Kronenbourg, please", or even just, "Kronenbourg, please"; that would be enough.'

'You're joking, aren't you? You're telling me that I have to say "please" to get a drink?' he asked in astonishment.

'No, I'm not joking, and yes, you do have to say "please" to get a drink in here,' I reiterated.

'OK; can I have a Kronenbourg, *please*?' he asked, in a sarcastic tone.

'No, you can't. You've got to ask properly first.'

'Can I have a Kronenbourg, please?' he asked, much more politely.

'Of course,' I replied, and went to pour his drink.

As I was pouring it, I heard him turn round and comment to Neilson and a couple of the others, 'I can't believe that. He just made me say "please" before he would serve me!'

'Well, did it hurt you?' Neilson demanded to know.

'Well... no, but...'

'No buts,' interrupted the strict Neilson. 'If you wanna be treated in the right way, then you should be polite to others.'

After he had paid for his drink and said 'thank you', he went straight up to Ged, who he knew. He repeated the same complaint to Ged, who basically repeated what Neilson had said to him.

Mo was interested in taking over the pub and had been coming in every night with a large group and putting a lot of money over the bar. The problem was that they would all drink in his café before coming over quite drunk. On one occasion, I was behind the bar, serving, when Mo and his entourage strolled in the pub. I immediately noticed that Mo was drinking from a large paper cup.

'Sorry, Mo, you can't drink that in here,' I told him.

'It's OK, I'll just drink it quickly,' he replied cockily.

'No, you won't. You're not drinking it in here,' I told him.

All his friends were watching, as they all seemed to have put him on a pedestal, probably because he was loaded and liked to play the 'big man'.

He lifted the cup up to his mouth and I gave him a final warning, 'If you drink any of that, I'm not serving you tonight!'

He drank the drink down in one and gave his audience a little grin. I felt like telling them all to clear off somewhere else, but managed to keep calm.

I served the others, while ignoring Mo. I then went to the other end of the bar to serve Eric and Daureen.

'Chris, can I have my usual?' Mo slurred.

'No, you can't.'

'Why not?'

'I told you I wouldn't serve you if you drank that drink in here, and you ignored me.'

'Are you telling me you're not serving me?' he demanded, loudly.

'That's exactly what I'm telling you.'

His mates were all gathered around him and he was clearly embarrassed.

'Look, Chris. I'm sorry I shouldn't have done that. But don't forget the bigger picture,' he said, referring to the possibility of his taking over the pub.

'I'm not forgetting the bigger picture, but I think you're forgetting that you don't run the pub yet. I'm still running it, and I'm telling you that you aren't getting a drink tonight,' I told him firmly.

He was shocked and disappointed and got up to leave,

followed by his 'gang'. Like Indian Mick, Clive and many others, he found out that money was not the be all and end all for us. There were more important things, like good manners and following the rules we had in the pub.

A few days after walking out of the pub for the last time, I met my accountant, Sid, at a nice pub at Strand on the Green, Chiswick. It was a lovely location, right by the Thames, and the customers appeared to have plenty of cash to throw around; they were not quibbling over five pence, like a few of our regulars always did!

It'd be all right running a pub like this, I was thinking. *No trouble, lovely area and a wealthy clientele.*

As I was thinking this, I became aware of a fat, bald man of about fifty propping up the bar. He did not look quite the full shilling and was really staring at two businessmen buying drinks at the bar. The two men carried their drinks over to a table, where they sat down and continued their conversation, all the time being watched by the bald man at the bar. As he got off his stool and made his way towards the men, I stood up, ready to intervene, when suddenly a voice in my head interrupted me.

What are you doing, Chris? It's not your problem any more, so let somebody else deal with it.

I did exactly as the voice advised; I sat back down and watched the events unfold in front of me.

'I bet that tastes good after a hard day at the office,' the man commented. 'I'm on my fifth pint, but I'll be having a few more before I go home.'

'Well, don't let me stop you,' replied one of the businessmen, who immediately continued his conversation with his colleague.

'Do you work round 'ere, then?' the bald man interrupted.

'Excuse me, do you mind? We're trying to have a private conversation here.'

'Oh, I do beg your pardon if I'm interrupting. I'll go back to the bar and leave you to continue your important conversation,'

The bald man looked like a sullen schoolkid as he sat there, glaring at the two businessmen. I knew that he would not be able to refrain from going over to them at least once more. He stared at them for a further twenty minutes before getting off his stool and approaching them once more.

'It's all go, innit?'

'Look, I've already told you we're trying to have a private conversation here, and—'

'Well, I'm trying to have a private conversation with you!' the bald man interrupted, to the astonishment of the businessmen. 'So don't you be so cheeky. You don't know who you are dealing with, do you?'

'No, we don't,' one of them replied, trying to appease him.

'Well, there you are, then. I'm only trying to have a conversation with you,' the bald man continued.

Thank God I don't have to deal with this rubbish any more, I thought to myself, and, at that moment, I realised there was no going back. This bald stranger had made me realise that, even in the nicest areas, you still have to deal with idiots and problems, and I had had a bellyful of them.

Printed in the United Kingdom
by Lightning Source UK Ltd.
124694UK00001B/67-315/A